Performance Appraisal and Career Development

The Personnel Management Series

Performance Appraisal and Career Development

Clive Fletcher and
Richard Williams

Stanley Thornes (Publishers) Ltd

First edition published in 1985 by Century Hutchinson Ltd

ISBN 0 09 158261 X

Second edition published in 1992 by:
Stanley Thornes (Publishers) Ltd
Old Station Drive
Leckhampton
CHELTENHAM GL53 0DN

British Library Cataloguing in Publication Data
Fletcher, Clive
    Performance appraisal and career development.
    – 2nd ed.
    I. Title   II. Williams, Richard
    658.30028

    ISBN 0–7487–1507–X

Typeset by Tech-Set, Gateshead, Tyne and Wear
Printed and bound in Great Britain at The Bath Press, Avon

Contents

1
Introduction: the wider context of performance appraisal

You will not find it in any of the textbooks on economics, but one of the great growth industries of the 1960s and early 1970s was performance appraisal. Many organizations introduced appraisal for the first time or revamped existing schemes. The typical scheme consisted of a written assessment of an individual's performance by a superior, followed by an interview in which the two parties discussed the written report and matters arising out of it. The purposes to which this assessment was put were nothing if not diverse – providing a basis for making comparisons between staff in deciding on promotion, pay increases or other incentives; acting as a motivating mechanism and as a vehicle for performance improvement, or collecting information for personnel planning and management development – these were all aims served by appraisal systems. In some cases the same scheme was supposed to achieve more than one or even all of these things. This is a pretty tall order by any standards, and appraisal has met with varying degrees of success. But most of the appraisal schemes are still with us, and are a central part of personnel management activity, linking in with almost every other aspect of the personnel function. Thus, appraisals can act as a partial check on the quality of the selection decisions being made in the organization's recruitment processes they can be one of the criteria for making promotion decisions or for singling out individuals who may have particularly high potential for development; they can be an important communication channel and action mechanism in bringing about training and development activities for individual employees. Appraisals can also feed basic information to the personnel division that will facilitate succession planning.

Small wonder, therefore, that such a central procedure, with so much weight loaded on to it, has received such great attention. Indeed, if the value of performance appraisal was measured in terms of the lip-service paid to the need for it, then appraisal schemes would surely be the most prized asset of any organization. In reality, the attitude to appraisal has been somewhat ambivalent. Some managers will agree that, in the abstract, appraisal is a 'good thing', but will treat the sight of an appraisal form awaiting completion with all the warmth they would show at the approach of a traffic warden when they were parked on a double yellow line. Sometimes the reasons for such reactions lie in the manager, but very often they lie in the appraisal scheme and the way it has been designed and introduced. In the harsher economic climate of the 1990s, performance appraisal faces a severe challenge and possibly only the well designed and well implemented schemes, with unequivocal support, will survive. Certainly, anything that demands resources, as appraisal does, will come under close scrutiny. We hope that the contents of this book will help anyone who will one day be running or setting up an appraisal system to do it in such a way as to increase its chances of surviving such evaluation.

At this point, however, it is necessary to emphasize that you are not looking at a 'DIY appraisal kit', though there are elements of that. Nor is it an academic text on the psychological principles involved in appraisal, with a detailed review of research and theory in the area. Instead, it is something between the two, attempting to bring together practical issues and problems of appraisal with the accumulated research findings on the subject. Too often, the academic and the practitioner seem to speak different languages of different worlds; we hope that this book is comprehensible to both. We also realize the danger of such an approach, but at least no one could accuse us of falling between two stools – we have dived headlong between them! A consequence of this kind of treatment of the subject is that no neat and clear solutions are on offer in these pages. The authors' biases will make themselves evident enough from time to time, but no prescription for *the best* appraisal scheme will be volunteered. There is, of course, no one 'right' way of operating appraisal schemes, just as there is no such thing as a perfect appraisal system – though to hear some managers talking you might be forgiven for thinking that perfection in this area is possible. Appraisals are only as good and as consistent in their effectiveness as the people using them, and it does not take a psychologist to tell you that that means you are going to find a lot of variation. But there are some general principles emerging that seem to give performance appraisal systems the greatest chance of being effective with a fair proportion of the managers and subordinates involved. These broad strategies are worth looking at, but you will still need a fair degree of tolerance with regard to ambiguity (a quality that should perhaps be written into the specifications for all personnel jobs).

Another aspect of the book needs a little explaining here. We are not exclusively concerned with appraisal practices here and now – though most of what is contained in these pages does concentrate on present day approaches. A little space is devoted to the evolution of appraisal. The reasons for taking this perspective are threefold: first, it helps us to understand how today's practices have been arrived at and why; second, an awareness of the problems encountered when trying earlier approaches is a useful safeguard against rediscovering the wheel; third, it shows how the theory and practice of appraisal are greatly influenced by the wider context of events – be they social, political, economic or scientific. This last point is particularly important, because, as was suggested earlier, this field of personnel management activity is entering what is likely to be a very difficult period of its development, and perhaps an appreciation of what has happened in the past will give us some clues as to what might happen in the future. Some of the content of the book takes what is necessarily a speculative look at what sort of changes performance appraisal might see in the next few years. And changes there will certainly be, if appraisal is to survive as a relevant activity. This is readily appreciated if we consider some of the social and economic developments of the day which provide the wider context for personnel practices.

- There are changes in social values. People are more concerned now than in the past about the quality of working life. And, arguably, they are more concerned to achieve a satisfactory balance amongst the various elements of their lives – for example, career and family.

- People are, in general, better educated and their occupational aspirations are higher. It is argued that employees at all levels within organizations want to have more of a say in the direction which their careers take.

- Economic growth is slower and there are fewer advancement opportunities for employees.

- Government intervention through anti-discrimination legislation and equal employment opportunity provisions has a continuing impact on company policies, as does the action of women and the minorities themselves.

- Rapid technological advances mean that jobs are disappearing or changing (so that they require different knowledge or skills). There consequently is a need for retraining or re-education to combat obsolescence.

All of these developments provide a challenge to those involved in devising or operating appraisal schemes, but the functions of appraisal, noted earlier (see page 1), will remain every bit as vital to organizations in the years ahead – in some ways, more so.

The intended readership of this book is chiefly students of personnel management, for whom it should provide a reasonably thorough survey of the major techniques and issues in the field. Where further information is required, fairly comprehensive references (both to basic and more specialized or technical sources) are given at the end of each chapter for the reader to follow up at will. However, experienced practitioners may also find the book useful as a statement of where we stand now and as a stimulus to their forward thinking and planning. And, we hope, the review of the less usual approaches to appraisal and career development, and of persisting issues in this area (based as far as possible on up-to-date findings and experience), will prove to be of some value to both students and practitioners alike.

These general points about the orientation of the book dealt with, the last thing to do is to map out the contents in a little more detail. The next chapter focuses on the history of performance appraisal (PA) and on the lessons of that history. Chapter 3 presents a picture of the typical modern British appraisal scheme and subjects it to a critical evaluation. As with most of the chapters, this embraces the career development (CD) aspects of appraisal as well – though that is an area requiring a book all of its own, and can be given only a limited treatment here. The fourth chapter looks at some of the less common approaches to appraisal and CD and assesses their strengths and weaknesses; international variations also are considered here and in other chapters - a not unimportant matter in view of the mobility of labour within the EEC. Chapter 5 concentrates on devising and implementing appraisal schemes, and on the key individual and organizational influences that have to be taken into account. The way appraisal meshes in with other personnel systems is also discussed. Logically enough, the next chapter (6) looks at the task of operating and maintaining the systems once they are up and running and gives some advice on evaluating and monitoring them. Chapter 6 also provides a yardstick against which to assess the results of any evaluation you might care to mount for yourself. The seventh chapter deals with a series of persisting issues in this field and, where possible, tries to draw some conclusions on the existing state of play – issues like whether giving performance feedback of a critical nature helps or hinders the appraisal process, the viability of self-appraisal, and so on. The next chapter (8) looks beyond the immediate horizons. Extrapolating from existing trends, it outlines the likely sources and dimensions of changes in PA and CD practices in the future. The final chapter summarizes and draws some tentative conclusions, as final chapters do.

2
Some formative influences on performance appraisal

To understand present performance appraisal practices and to make some reasonable guesses about what the future holds in this area, we really need to cast a look backwards and see how we arrived here in the first place. In other words, we need to comprehend how and why ideas and techniques in the field of appraisal evolved in the way they did. This is no easy task, as there are many influences to take into account. Some changes have come about through shifts in society as a whole, some through the influence of research, and many have come from the ideas and innovations of individual practitioners and organizations. Trying to unravel exactly who contributed to what, and when, would be a laborious exercise and one of dubious value for present purposes. What follows is one brief *interpretation* – and that word is used advisedly – of the way appraisal has developed, charting the major trends in theory and practice. These perspectives from the past provide some useful lessons for us today, but, before we consider these, we have to go through a short history lesson.

Beginnings

People have been making informal appraisals of each other's performance for about as long as the human race has indulged in group activities. Fortunately, however, we do not need to go back quite that far to trace the roots of the formal appraisal systems of today. The interest in job evaluation techniques following the First World War is as good a place to start as any. This interest, an American rather than a British phenomenon, seems to have quickly led to the logical step of evaluating the people doing the jobs. But in the 1920s and 1930s this was limited chiefly to managers and how to identify those amongst them who had potential for development. During that period, American industry paid considerable attention to developments in psychology and introduced the use of psychological tests and aptitude surveys. One of the reasons for this was a desire to raise the morale of the workforce, the assumption being that high morale led to high productivity – a notion reinforced by the famous Hawthorne studies, which, in retrospect, seem to have been interpreted (wrongly) in such a way as to fit in with the prevailing social outlook of the time.[1] Another prevalent and ill-founded assumption was that the goals of the individual and of the organization were in harmony. These notions persisted into the 1950s, as did the practice of appraising personality rather than performance or ability. The reasons behind this emphasis on personality seem mainly to have been the difficulty of evaluating executive performance and the perceived need of managers to possess human relations skills in order to be effective leaders; these are much the same reasons as one finds today when looking at appraisal systems that still incorporate trait ratings, though perhaps no longer with the implication that such attributes are innate and have to be identified and developed through appraisal.

All that has been said so far relates to America. In Britain, things appear to have got off to a slower start, although there was some early interest in morale, as evidenced by developments taking place within management education. The application of Taylor's scientific management was recognized as a potential source of industrial unrest, and managerial skill on the part of engineers in their dealings with shop stewards was seen as necessary for good labour relations. As for appraisal, this was seen as an incentive-linked activity, the incentive being promotion. This characteristic of the early appraisal schemes of the 1930s was still evident in the 1950s, but gradually some American influence crept in and much greater attention was given to management development. In both countries importance was attached to giving feedback – letting the individual know where he or she stood. The reasons behind this differed, though: in the UK it was to make people realize they were being noticed and to thus give them an incentive to work harder; whereas in the USA the thinking was still that happy workers are productive workers and that knowing where you stood made you happier.

The late 1950s and the early 1960s

By the late 1950s, appraisal systems on both sides of the Atlantic were characterized by use of the rating method and a focus on personality traits. The extent and sophistication of the schemes was far greater in the USA than in the UK,[2] and the history of appraisal is very largely an American one, for from the late 1950s there followed a series of developments that mostly had no parallel in Britain but which shaped appraisal practices in both countries. The first of these was Douglas McGregor's famous article in the Harvard Business Review entitled 'An Uneasy Look at Performance Appraisal', which was published in 1957.[3] He pinpointed the reluctance of managers to give critical feedback to subordinates and said that much of this stemmed from having to make judgements about personality traits – the appraisers felt that they were 'playing God' and found this to be unacceptable. McGregor was giving voice to a rising tide of doubt on the conventional approach to appraisal, supported by social scientists who queried the value of letting people know where they stood when in so many cases the individual was just getting a demotivating thumbs-down. McGregor suggested a switch away from appraising personality and towards job performance, incorporating Drucker's *Management by Objectives* – the individual should be assessed against set goals. Drawing on the various psychological and sociological studies of the effects of participation, McGregor advocated a more participative approach to appraisal, with a strong element of self-appraisal. The role of the appraiser was more that of 'helper' than that of 'judge' – in other words to assist the individual in the formulation of his own goals and in assessing the extent to which they had been reached. The whole appraisal became more future-orientated than had previously been the case.

Much of the research on appraisal that came some time after McGregor wrote his article has largely vindicated his views. Somewhat similar ideas were expressed by Norman Maier in a book[4] in which he described the defensive reactions that criticism elicited in appraisees and how this reduced the chances of getting constructive post- appraisal action. He advocated a participative, problem-solving approach to appraisal in which both parties identified the problems associated with the job in the past year and together worked out solutions to them, with the onus being on the appraisee to provide most of the solutions. The rationale for this was that appraisees were more likely to implement action plans that they themselves had devised. Maier was perhaps even more emphatic than McGregor had been on the incompatibility of the roles of judge and of helper that appraisers were being asked to fulfil in their interviews. You could do a 'Tell and Sell' interview, as he called it, which gave the appraisees feedback and left them knowing where they stood and, in all probability, feeling defensive and disinclined to take any remedial action over their supposed deficiencies. Alternatively, you could carry out a problem-solving type of interview which produced changes in behaviour that might well improve performance but which would leave the appraisee (happily?) unaware of the way his or her performance was viewed. What you could not do with any degree of success, said Maier, was both together in the same interview.

Maier was supported in the 1960s by a series of research studies carried out by Herbert Meyer and his colleagues in the General Electric Company of America.[5] These seminal investigations confirmed that appraisal interviews which sought to both give feedback and produce an increase in subordinate motivation (and thus in performance) tended to reduce motivation and brought little or no change in behaviour.

Criticism in the interview seemed particularly damaging and unhelpful, especially if the appraisal was linked to rewards (chiefly pay). They advocated, on the basis of their studies, that pay should be separated from the appraisal as far as possible – it simply promoted more defensiveness on the appraisee's part – and that a series of work-planning and review sessions should be held. These differed from traditional appraisals in that

a   there were more frequent discussions of performance
b   no summary judgements or ratings were made
c   as noted, salary action discussions were held separately
d   the accent was on participative goal-setting and problem-solving, in line with the ideas of Maier and McGregor.

The General Electric studies were very influential, partly because they built on and confirmed earlier writers' views, and partly because they were probably the first comprehensive series of investigations of this kind; much of what had been done before this was research on the inadequacies of rating methods and how to improve them. The advice of Meyer and his colleagues had an echo (a trifle belatedly) in this country in the work of Randell.[6] We shall see later that some of Meyer's conclusions stand the test of time better than others do.

So by the end of the 1960s a considerable change had taken place in the thinking on appraisal. It was realized that in appraisal the goals of the organization and the individual were not necessarily the same. Performance feedback was no longer assumed to produce either more satisfied or more effective subordinates. Appraisal of performance and goal-setting increasingly took over from assessment of personality as the main focus of the exercise. And there was a greater awareness of the fact that traditional appraisal practice had been trying to achieve too much and that the link with pay systems was probably counter-productive. Finally, the virtues of a more participative, problem-solving approach were being realized.

The 1970s

Much of the research on appraisal in the 1970s supported and elaborated on the conclusions reached in the 1960s rather than produced any fundamentally new directions. In practice, two inter-connected trends were evident – greater openness in reporting, and a higher degree of subordinate participation in the appraisal process.[7] These were in part a progression of the liberalization of social attitudes of the 1960s, but government decisions played a role as well, particularly in America. The Employment Protection Act in the UK and the Freedom of Information Act in the US both required that the individual be allowed to see what was written about him or her, though in the UK legislation this was confined to cases where unsatisfactory performance was liable to lead to dismissal. Assessment practices in general were further influenced in America by the equal opportunities laws and regulations which placed appraisal schemes under public scrutiny of a kind which they had not hitherto been used to and which involved having to prove (when challenged) that the schemes were appropriate, fair and equitable. A multitude of court cases ensued where these attributes were called into question – often successfully.[8] The most dismal aspect of all this is that the legislation was only demanding of appraisal practices what they should have been achieving anyway. The equivalent equal opportunity apparatus in Britain does not seem to have had the same impact, though potentially it could.

The other notable development of the period was the rise of trade union interest in appraisal practices. As the unions themselves became more powerful, and as managerial staff were increasingly drawn into organized associations of one form or another, appraisal was seen as a legitimate focus of union concern. This was boosted by the series of Government pay policies and, more specifically, pay 'freezes' that characterized these economically difficult times. When pay was taken out of the negotiating arena for long periods, it was not surprising to find that, like nature, trade unions abhor a vacuum and that they turned their attention to other matters which might otherwise have come lower down on their agenda (if they ever got on it at all). The effect of this was to make performance appraisals yet more visible and open to challenge, with the consequence (amongst other things) that the pressure for openness and subordinate participation was heightened.

So much for the potted history of appraisal. We will consider various issues raised in it – conflicting goals, performance feedback and its effects, the consequences of open reporting and the impact of legislation – at different points in subsequent chapters. What we shall do here, though, is go into more detail on the merits of the rating method, a technique much used throughout the period described – especially in the early days of appraisal – and still in evidence now. When that has been dealt with, we shall round off by making some general observations on the development of appraisal aims and methods.

The rating method

While early appraisal schemes suffered from difficulties over what they were assessing and why, a lot of their problems stemmed also from the 'how' of appraisal, which for the most part consisted of rating methods.

The use of rating scales was consistent with the purposes of these earlier systems in that they facilitated comparisons between staff that served as a basis for identifying high flyers or for giving incentives. All too often the qualities rated were those personality traits that a few senior managers felt were the most important and significant for the exercise of effective leadership. This is obviously a subjective and rather haphazard approach and it is not surprising that different managers had different ideas on the qualities needed. A more rational method is to base the rating scales on the outcome of a carefully conducted job analysis, the main elements of the job being incorporated into the appraisal form – but the thinking on appraisal had not progressed to this stage until the late 50s and early 60s (and even now, where job-related activities or abilities are rated, they are frequently *not* arrived at via such a methodical procedure). Apart from the fact that it offers some way of grading people, the rating method does have other advantages:

- It is flexible and can be tailored to fit all sorts of situations and jobs. Indeed, to be used properly, it must be tailored to fit the task assessed;

- It encourages an analytical view of the subordinate's performance, providing an emphasis on how results are achieved rather than just on the results themselves.

These advantages are, however, outweighed by the problems rating scales present – some of which are inherent in the technique and some simply reflect the way the scales are used. The chief difficulties are as follows:

1   *The problem of subjectivity.* Whilst there is a subjective element in all techniques of performance appraisal, it seems particularly evident in the use of ratings. There are two aspects. First, the rater often makes assessments on scales that are too impressionistic and insufficiently tied to evidence; it is almost too 'easy' to give a rating. We then get phenomena like the 'halo' effect, where one quality of an individual is judged very favourably and is allowed to colour the assessor's ratings of other qualities. (So much for the analytical approach that the method might encourage!) Second, the scales themselves are open to differing interpretations. This is often the result of inadequate definition of the scale end points or interval points, but to some extent it is an unavoidable aspect of the technique, which imposes dimensions of assessment upon the rater rather than letting him use his own. The ratings he is asked to use may not represent the way he thinks about an individual's performance at all, or may be interpreted quite differently by different assessors (try getting different people to define 'drive', 'integrity', 'maturity' and 'determination' and you will frequently get quite significantly different concepts emerging). All this has the inevitable consequence of variable standards of assessment being

operated, which undermines (at least in part) the comparability function of many rating scales.

2   One of the aims of rating scales is to achieve a meaningful discrimination of varying levels of performance amongst staff. Unfortunately it is very common to find that appraisers do not distribute their ratings very widely or evenly; they show either a central tendency (putting most people in the middle of the scale) or a positively skewed rating (almost everyone rated very favourably). For example, in one organization[9] the overall performance ratings were distributed like this:

	%
Outstanding	4
Very good	50.5
Good	39
Fair	6.5
Not quite adequate	0.5
Unsatisfactory	0

Two possible reasons for this come to mind. One is that appraisers are reluctant to be critical and thus mark subordinates rather favourably in order to avoid conflict with them. The other is that, in most organizations, unsatisfactory employees are dismissed or leave of their own accord fairly quickly and the rest of the workforce do a good job in general, and this is reflected in the assessments. Probably both of these factors contribute to the kind of rating distributions we see, but none the less the effect is to reduce the value of rating scales as a means of differentiating performance levels.

3   The third problem is that rating scales often do not reflect the attributes necessary for effective performance in the job. As was pointed out earlier, appropriate use of the method implies that different rating scales be used for different jobs. But for the sake of comparability, and perhaps for simplicity, organizations often apply the same scales to large numbers of people doing quite different work. They sometimes use methods to try to get round the disadvantages of this (for example, by leaving some additional blank rating scales for appraisers to fill in their own dimensions, or by getting the appraiser to indicate whether each quality is rated of high, medium or low relevance to the job concerned), but the whole exercise is devalued irrespective of these attempts. This is, of course, a problem of the improper *use* of scales rather than of the method as such, but even where scales are properly tailored to the particular job it could be argued that they never adequately reflect the complex behaviour required to fill the managerial role effectively.

All of these problems (and some more not mentioned here) beset early appraisal schemes, and they are still present today. A number of ways of trying to get round them have been devised, with varying degrees of success. We shall look at some of the main ones in later chapters. For a more technical discussion of rating methods see Landy and Farr[10] and Handyside.[11]

Some observations on the development of appraisal practice

The changes that have taken place in the field of performance appraisal over the period reviewed illustrate the fact that activities in this area reflect wider changes in society as a whole. Early appraisal schemes enshrined a view of employees that now would be regarded as overly simplistic (and possibly by some as optimistic), but which were in keeping with the more authoritarian outlook of the time and with the assumptions that might be made in a society where the memory of the Great Depression was still fresh. Against such a background, believing that the individual needed and wanted to be told how he or she was doing and what needed improvement, that the individual would see his or her aspirations as being consistent with the needs of the organization, and that the appraisal system would be the vehicle for both the carrot (if you do well you will be noticed and rewarded) and the stick (if you are falling down, that too will be noticed), all seemed quite reasonable. People were expected to have faith in the fairness and efficiency of the appraisal system because they had faith in their superiors who operated it.

This rather naive set of assumptions was eroded by a world war (always good for shaking up attitudes) and a gradual rise in economic prosperity. The latter afforded greater choice and freedom of employment, not to mention an increased sense of security. By the mid-1960s a considerably more liberal social outlook prevailed, along with higher expectations both in terms of material and psychological well-being. Research in the social sciences had shown that the relationship between job satisfaction and productivity was by no means a straightforward one, and that organizations were infinitely more complex than had previously been thought. At a more fundamental level, the notion that abilities were primarily inherited rather than acquired – an issue epitomized by the debate between those psychologists who believed in a concept of general intelligence and those who did not – was increasingly challenged and modified. Together these shifts led to appraisal schemes of a very different character. The emphasis was no longer on identifying the 'born leaders' or on using appraisal as a crude instrument for organizational goals. Instead, appraisal became more of an opportunity for the subordinate to communicate and to influence, more orientated to the future than to the past, and more concerned with developing the potential in the majority rather than in the minority. The dominant theme was more akin to counselling than to managerial assessment.

As society has become more open and less rigid, so has appraisal. It has gone from being the sole concern of top management to being something that the appraisees, the trade unions, and, in an indirect way, even governments have a say in. It has become a highly 'public' activity. The tendency for the government to intervene in all sorts of areas in the 1970s did not leave performance appraisal unscathed and it remains to be seen whether the full implications of the legislation for appraisal practices will eventually be realized here as they have been in America. The main point to be made, however, is that if one accepts that the appraisal field mirrors many of the social, political and psychological beliefs and attitudes of its time (and, of course, the interpretation given here can only be a subjective one), then we should be able to make some projections about how appraisal might develop in the years ahead. What, for example, will be the impact of further prolonged economic recession, high 'structural' unemployment, and the increased use of microprocessors and other advanced technology? How will appraisal and career development adapt to the changing concepts of intelligence, the increasing evidence that human abilities *do* fluctuate over time, and that some attributes previously thought to be necessary for effective managerial performance might actually militate against it? But having glanced at the past, and before looking into the future, we shall turn now to the present.

Summary

To provide some insights as to how present appraisal practices have arisen, this chapter has looked back over the history of appraisal. Early appraisal systems in the UK emphasized the importance of incentives. In the 1950s such systems typically involved ratings of personality traits, but this approach to appraisal came under increasing attack. Part of the problem was the rating method itself, which tended to be highly subjective and consequently suffered from a variety of defects. Other problems identified were that letting people know where they stand in the course of an appraisal often just reduces their motivation and puts the appraiser in conflicting roles (judge versus helper). Research by Meyer seemed to support these conclusions and indicated that more could be achieved if appraisal was kept separate from pay and was tied to goal-setting. By the end of the 1960s, performance appraisal was generally seen as a more participative, problem-solving process concentrated on task performance rather than personality. The following decade saw an even greater shift towards openness and participation in appraisal, reflecting changes in society as a whole. Beliefs about the nature of human abilities, theories of motivation, trade union concerns, government legislation and changing social attitudes have all influenced and modified performance appraisal practices and are likely to continue doing so.

References

1 D. Bramel and R. Friend, 'Hawthorne, the myth of the docile worker and class bias in psychology', *American Psychologist*, **36** (1981), pp. 867–78.

2 R. Stewart, 'Management development: Some American Comparisons', *The Manager* (January 1957).

3 D. McGregor, 'An uneasy look at performance appraisal,' *Harvard Business Review*, **35** (1957), pp. 89–94.

4 N.R.F. Maier, 'Three types of appraisal interview', *Personnel* (March/April 1958), pp. 27–40.

5 H.H. Meyer, E. Kay and J.R.P. French, Jr., 'Split roles in performance appraisal', *Harvard Business Review*, **43** (1965), pp. 123–9.

6 G.A. Randell, P.M.A. Packard, R.L. Shaw and A.J. Slater *Staff Appraisal*, Institute of Personnel Management 1974).

7 D. Gill, B. Ungerson and M. Thakur, *Performance Appraisal in Perspective*, IPM Information Report, **14** (Institute of Personnel Management 1973).
   D. Gill, *Appraising Performance: Present Trends and the Next Decade*, IPM Information Report, **25** (Institute of Personnel Management 1977).
   J. Walker, C. Fletcher, R.Williams and K. Taylor. 'Performance appraisal: an open or shut case?', *Personnel Review*, **6** (1977), pp. 38–42.
   R. Williams, J. Walker and C. Fletcher, 'International review of staff appraisal practices: current trends and issues', *Public Personnel Management* (January/February, 1977) pp. 5–12.

8 W.H. Holley and H.S. Feild, 'Performance appraisal and the law', *Labor Law Journal*, **26** (1975), pp. 423–30.
   D.B. Schneier, 'The impact of EEO legislation on performance appraisals.' *Personnel*, **55** (1978), pp. 24–34.

9 E. Anstey, C. Fletcher and J. Walker, *Staff Appraisal and Development* (Allen and Unwin 1976).

10 F.J. Landy and J.L. Farr, *The Measurement of Work Performance* (Academic Press 1983).

11 J.D. Handyside, 'On ratings and rating scales', in P. Herriot (ed.), *Assessment and Selection in Organizations* (Wiley 1989).

3
The state of the art

In the previous chapter we looked at the rise of performance appraisal practices and the main influences on them. With that background, it is now possible to examine where we are today – the present state of the art.

Over the past 20 years several surveys of appraisal practices and trends have been carried out.[1] From these it is possible to build up a fairly clear picture of what is and what is not typical in this area. There is, of course, considerable variation, which is only to be expected with different organizations trying to meet different needs, but the similarities none the less outweigh the differences. At the end of this chapter several case study examples are given of performance appraisal and career development schemes that represent the usual range of approaches one finds. But to illustrate the most characteristic features of the prevailing UK appraisal practices, and to analyse their strengths and weaknesses, we will adopt the device of creating an 'Identikit' appraisal system, that is, describe a fictitious system that is made up of all the most commonly found features, and then go on to examine and evaluate it.

The Identikit picture of a British appraisal system

Aims   The aims of the scheme are nothing if not numerous, with as many as six or seven different purposes being served. But the main ones are:
1   To help improve current performance.
2   To set and review performance objectives.
3   To assess training and development needs.

Who decides   The designation of these aims, and indeed the thinking behind the whole system, has come chiefly from within Personnel. The Training and Development Manager has been particularly heavily involved, with the Personnel Director taking overall authority and, in consultation with some of his colleagues, having the final say.

Periodicity	The appraisals operate on an annual basis.
Level of appraiser	The individual's immediate superior is the appraiser; 'grandfather' (the manager two levels up) sees the report, adds his signature and any comments he thinks necessary.
Coverage	The annual appraisals take in everyone from senior management to first level supervisors. Increasingly, clerical and secretarial staff are being covered and there has been some move towards including skilled manual workers. And there are schemes which now apply to directors.
Training	Most of the appraisers have been given some training; this consists of a written guide to the purpose and procedures of the organization's appraisal system, and a brief training course on appraisal interviewing.
Contents of the appraisal	The report form itself runs to four sides. The first the appraisal page is devoted to biographical details of the job-holder and a job description. The second page requires the appraiser to list the objectives the individual has been working towards over the last year and to comment (in a free-written form) on the extent to which these have been achieved. On the third page there is a section for the appraiser to identify any obstacles to the improvement of the appraisee's performance and to suggest how these might be overcome. Then comes the overall rating of performance – a seven point scale from 'poor' to 'outstanding'. Following this is a section for the appraiser to comment on the individual's training and development needs. A brief section for the appraiser to add general comments and another for the appraisee to sign the form and to add any comment, if he sees fit, complete the third page. The fourth and last page of the form – the only one the appraisee does not see – commences with the appraiser's ratings of the job-holder's present promotability and long-term potential, along with supporting comments. The rest of the page is devoted to the 'grandfather's' report; he is invited to state his agreement or disagreement with the ratings given, and to comment generally on the appraisee's performance over the period under review.

The appraisal interview   As already indicated, the appraisee is shown the part of the report dealing with present performance, and has the opportunity to discuss that and other issues in the appraisal interview. Held annually with his immediate superior, this lasts on average around half an hour and, apart from discussing the content of the form, will range over the objectives for the next year. Issues of promotion and potential may be discussed, but generally the appraisers try to avoid these.

Use of the appraisal   Finally, the report form is sent on to Personnel where it is monitored for any action recommendations that need looking at centrally (for example, on transfers). It will, of course, be referred to when personnel decisions have to be made (for example, on short listings for promotion), and at the salary review period which follows three to six months after the appraisal; the appraisal rating will have some input to the salary decision taken then, but it is only one of several factors taken into account in fixing the level of increments.

The strengths and weaknesses, and pros and cons, of the typical British appraisal scheme

Having described the 'Identikit' scheme, we can now look at it in more detail and subject it to an appraisal all of its own. We start first with the aims of the scheme and how they are decided on, which is of course fundamental to the whole exercise and where the roots of many of the problems that beset appraisal are found. A great deal more will be said about the need for consultation and participation of various groups at the design stage of appraisal systems in Chapter 5. For the moment it is sufficient to note that too narrow a range of interest and opinion tends to be represented in the formulation of such systems. However, the aims of the typical appraisal scheme do reflect a balance between the needs of the organization and the needs of the appraisee, even if the balance is tilted rather more in the direction of the former. Taken individually, any of the three aims mentioned is quite reasonable and legitimate for an appraisal system; the trouble is that, taken together, they give the appearance of trying to be all things to all men. The problems that arise from having too many aims, some of which may conflict with one another, have already been alluded to, and are generally well documented.[2] The main potential conflict is between the assessment and reward aspects, on the one hand, and the motivating and counselling aspects, on the other – the appraiser is left with the difficult task of reconciling the roles of judge and of helper.[3] This is an issue which we shall have cause to return to at a number of points in the following pages.

The periodicity of appraisal is one of the features least likely to vary from one organization to another. Whilst there might be good reason for adopting more frequent review sessions where the appraisal has an element of goal-setting, it is as much as most companies can do to get their managers to do the appraisals reliably on an annual basis. And as long as the appraisal is allied to adequate day-to-day supervision this seems quite reasonable. The decision to leave the main part of the task to the appraisee's immediate boss is also logical enough. 'Father' should know his subordinate's work better than anyone else (apart from the subordinate of course), and if the latter is to see the report and have a chance to discuss it, then 'Father' is also the best person to conduct the appraisal interview. Some organizations opt for grandfather-level appraisal, which has the virtues of ensuring that managers two levels up know what is going on below them, and of giving the appraisees a second opinion, which they may feel to be more objective (though it may not actually be so).

The coverage of the appraisal is quite wide, but one could argue that it is still not wide enough. Some continue to exclude top management leading to the inevitable danger that those lower down the line will say to themselves 'Well, if it is no use to them, why should it be of any use to me?' Leaving out skilled manual staff does not seem entirely wise either: have they got no scope for improving their performance? Have they no ideas on how to make things run more effectively in their area of work? Do they not need any formal recognition of work done well, or not so well? Are none of them possessed of potential for higher level work if developed? (For the experience of one organization that gave a degree of appraisal coverage to those at clerical levels, see Anstey, Fletcher and Walker.[4])

The Identikit appraisal system is weak on training. Despite the fact that most organizations do provide some training, only a minority provide anything like adequate training, particularly in the skills of appraisal interviewing.

Moving on to the contents of the appraisal form, the first thing to say is that the length is about right – more than one appraisal scheme has sunk beneath the threshold of management tolerance through being too paper-laden.

The allocation of a major part of the form to objectives and assessment of how far they have been met reflects the popularity of this approach over recent years. Its popularity is such that some organizations seem to manage to delude themselves that they are using it when in fact they are not, according to a study by Holdsworth.[5] However, to briefly reiterate its advantages:

a It offers a more objective yardstick by which an individual's performance can be measured.
b Goal-setting sessions are effective motivators and engender less defensiveness on the part of the appraisee.
c It is job-related by nature.
d Setting and reviewing objectives makes a review of the job and its priorities inevitable.

In view of the problems encountered with the rating method which we looked at earlier, it is not surprising to find that the results-orientated appraisal technique was increasing its popularity still further in the late 1970s. However, there are some considerable difficulties with it, the main ones being:

1 By itself, it offers no scope for making quantifiable comparisons between employees for use in reward decisions.

2 Not all aspects of a job are specifiable in terms of objectives – indeed, sometimes very little is. Even where this does not rule out appraising the job in this way, concentrating solely on those elements that can be cast in terms of targets may lead to the neglect of other important elements, and thus to an unduly pragmatic emphasis on ends rather than means.

3 Sometimes circumstances change quickly and make goals out of date or inappropriate before the time comes to review them (though this can be offset by holding more frequent review sessions).

4 The individual may not have sufficient control over his environment to be sure that achievement of goals is dependent purely on his own performance. In fact, this is almost always the case in large, complex organizations.[6] Some schemes try to build-in a recognition of this. While this helps, it does not overcome the problem of trying to assess someone in terms of achieving objectives that are not entirely within his control; the extent to which other factors have influenced performance and whether the individual could really have controlled them brings the discussion firmly back into the realm of the subjective.

5 The goals to be achieved can vary in level of difficulty from appraisee to appraisee. Setting goals is a collaborative effort between appraiser and appraisee. It is not unknown for goals simply to become euphemisms for minimum standards of performance; appraisees do not often went to commit themselves to achieving difficult targets, and appraisers sometimes collude with them in setting objectives that are too easily achieved so as to avoid any difficulties that may arise from discussion of failure to achieve them. So, the standards against which people are assessed may

vary considerably, and sometimes the standards are not as high as might reasonably be expected.

6   While goal setting may be more effective in terms of one of the organization's needs, that is motivating staff, it does not necessarily fulfil one of the appraisee's needs from appraisal, namely that of getting feedback. Indeed, this is claimed as one of its strengths in so far as it does not elicit defensive reactions. However, it is not quite as black-and-white as this; if the individual has not achieved his or her goals fully, some discussion of the reason why should take place, and this may lead the appraisal into the contentious area of critical feedback.

Any detailed examination of results-orientated approaches quickly brings to light elements of subjectivity that are sometimes played down by advocates of this kind of appraisal. However, it does offer a quite different technique from rating methods and has its own marked advantages.

It was noted above that the section on obstacles to the improvement of the appraisee's performance can have the purpose of recognizing potential external limitations to goal achievement. However, it can also represent the organization's wish to have things both ways – both an objective-setting orientation *and* a chance for appraisers to comment on the limitations of the appraisee himself. Even if the section is not quite as described in our Identikit scheme, there is very often something which has a similar purpose – that is, of allowing the appraiser to comment more specifically on the appraisee's weaknesses.

There is also an element of having one's cake and eating it about the use of the overall rating of performance. Organizations are aware of the difficulties of the rating method and have decreased their use of it, but most of them still want to include some grading procedures to facilitate fair and equitable reward policies. So, the overall rating of performance, with all its inherent problems, is included in most appraisal forms as a vehicle for summarizing the assessment and for making comparisons between employees; see Example 3.1 for some illustrations of typical rating scale formats in use at present. Much the same can be said of the ratings on promotability and potential but, along with the other career development aspects of appraisal, this will be commented on separately below.

During the 70s and 80s there was a significant shift towards openness and even towards an element of appraisee participation in the appraisal process.[8] The usual thing is for the appraisee to see what is written about present performance and often to be allowed to comment on it if he or she wishes; this freedom does not, however, generally extend to ratings of potential. While openness is widely regarded as a 'good thing'

Example 3.1 *Illustrations of rating scale formats*

There are four main types of rating scale used. (For a full survey of the variations on these themes, see Landy and Farr.[7])

1 *Scales with verbally described intervals, e.g.*

Overall performance

Outstanding	Very good	Good	Fair	Not quite adequate	Unsatisfactory
☐	☐	☐	☐	☐	☐

2 *Numerical (or alphabetical) ratings* The individual is rated on a number of criteria using a scale ranging from best to worst, with a number or letter given to each interval point, e.g.

Oral expression

High   Low
1   2   3   4   5

3 *Graphic rating scales* These generally dispense with formal interval points apart from the two extremes and the middle, but define in some detail the behaviour associated with the quality being rated, e.g.

a Follows instructions
b Completes work on time
c Is punctual and regular in attendance
d Does not require excessive supervision

High ├──────────┼──────────┤ Low

4 *Comparative scales* The individual is rated on some quality in terms of his standing relative to others of his level, e.g.

Initiative

a Not as good as the great majority
b OK, but many I have known have been better
c Typical of the middle group
d Better than most, though I have known better
e One of the best I have known

and as ethically desirable, it can also offer a threat to the validity of the whole process – appraisers being afraid to give their honest opinions in case anything unfavourable is objected to by the appraisee. This is a major and continuing issue in the field and touches on the aims of the whole exercise. However, whatever the problems of openness and participation, most organizations seem to have perceived greater objections to running 'closed' reporting systems, though this is less true in the public sector.[9]

The inclusion of free-written sections for both 'father' and 'grand-father' to add whatever observations they see fit is something of a catch-all device, but a fairly reasonable one. Like the essay method of appraisal, these sections have the virtue of flexibility and of letting the writers say what *they* think is important, but such contributions have no value in terms of comparing staff reported on and are highly subjective and dependent on the writer's ability to express himself or herself on paper.

The provision of appraisal interviews is certainly a strong point of the scheme – at least, potentially. There is no doubt that, properly done, these interviews can achieve a great deal in the eyes of both appraiser and appraisee; there is equally little doubt that if mishandled they will be an embarrassing and fruitless use of time.[10] This is the point at which the crunch comes for most appraisers, where the appraisee has to be given some idea of where he or she stands in such a way as to motivate and help rather than to discourage. It makes more demands on the manager's skill than any other aspect of appraisal, and all too often the training given is not adequate to meet these needs.

The final stages of the appraisal scheme see the report being sent on to Personnel. A copy of the report may or may not be kept by the appraiser. For a results-orientated appraisal of this kind there is a very good case for letting him or her keep a copy to review progress against objectives at regular intervals. The other side of the argument, though, is that if no copy of last year's report is available, there may be less of a tendency for appraisers to try to maintain a false impression of continuity – the temptation to show that the opinions expressed last year were correct and that what has happened subsequently is in line with them. Personnel's use of the form for career development purposes is dealt with below, but the last point one might make here about our appraisal scheme is that it has heeded the numerous warnings on tying it too closely to pay (unlike many American schemes where the appraisal has a direct and fairly immediate relationship with pay); this is definitely a plus point.

Appraisal and career development

That our Identikit appraisal scheme is intimately linked with career development is clear from all of the aims mentioned on page 15. And, as the Identikit description has shown, those aims are reflected in the report form. Taking a broad view of career development – which emphasizes development within the job and not just the more traditional notions of upward advancement – it is only to be expected that the appraisal scheme is a basic foundation for many development activities. The remainder of this chapter will illustrate some of the interrelationships between the typical appraisal system and other career development systems. Since the prevailing appraisal system is, in essence, a *management* appraisal system, we will concentrate on management development, viewing this as career development directed at a particular category of employees. Drawing on several sources,[11] we portray the basic characteristics of management development in Britain today, again using the 'Identikit' device.

Aims

While the details of policies vary from organization to organization, there is a fair degree of agreement that management development concerns improving current managerial performance and providing a pool of managerial talent for the future. Organizational effectiveness is the primary consideration, but there is usually some recognition of individual needs and that these should in some way be balanced with those of the organization. Though not always stated explicitly, management development is often seen as a system or function of the organization and as a responsibility of all managers.

Who decides?

Most probably, top management plays a key role in determining the policy, whereas implementation is likely to be in the hands of a specialist manager, in Personnel or Training. As we shall see, however, other parties play some part in the implementation of management development.

Coverage

In most organizations the management development arrangements are likely to apply to all managerial employees. A significant minority of organizations take a narrow view, applying management development to certain levels only. Also, there is a tendency for employers to concentrate training on their more recent employees, rather than on their experienced managers.

Assessing managerial potential

The appraisal system is almost universally used as one means of assessing potential. However, it is rare for managers to be given any guidance on the criteria they are to use in making their assessments. The assessment of promotability and potential is usually part of the 'closed' section of the report form. Some organizations draw a distinction between the assessment of promotability (perhaps defined in terms of readiness for promotion) and that of potential. And ratings of potential tend to fall into two categories: assessment of level of responsibility expected to be reached (possibly expressed in terms of the organization's grading structure), or assessments of when the potential will be realizable (usually expressed as a number of years). Sometimes the different types may be combined into some sort of composite rating. The rating(s) may be supported by some kind of written justification. The use of psychological tests or simulation techniques, either separately or in combination, has increased.

Promotion procedures

The most usual way of filling management positions is by internal promotion, and it is common for succession-planning machinery to be linked to the promotion system. Internal advertising is frequently used to identify suitable candidates. Confidential reports by line managers are likely to play a part in contributing to promotion decisions but, aside from the appraisal report, the most commonly used tool is the interview. There are likely to be at least two interviews, probably individual rather than by a panel. Recent job performance and achievement and career progression are said to be the main criteria underlying promotion decisions.

Identifying training and development needs

Again, the appraisal system is a principal method. Quite apart from this, the manager's boss may be consulted about training needs and many organizations claim they consult the prospective trainee.

Training and development methods

A frequently stated aim of appraisal schemes is to improve current performance, and they therefore constitute a major developmental tool. Other on-the-job methods that are widely used include coaching, job rotation, and projects. Off-the-job methods will most probably be in-house or external training courses. Higher level managers are more likely to attend external courses whereas the more junior managers are more likely to go on internal courses. The boss, probably with someone else, will take the decision about attending an off-the-job course, but the subordinate is unlikely to participate in the decision. The most widely used training programmes are in the areas of general, staff and financial management.

The strengths and weaknesses, and pros and cons, of the typical British management development system

Earlier, we criticized the aims of performance appraisal on the grounds that the interests of some of the parties concerned were insufficiently considered by the policy-making body. With the somewhat broader management development policy, the picture is slightly different in that the level of decision-making authority is higher and there appears to be much greater involvement by top management in policy formulation.[12] However, as with performance appraisal, some of the principal consumers – for example, managers due to receive training – tend not to play a part in the decision-making. Thus, despite what the policies may say, there is in practice a bias towards the organizational objectives of management development, with the needs of the individual manager being a secondary consideration.

To the extent that it is *management* development which is under scrutiny here, it might be thought odd to challenge those systems which fail to consider non-managerial employees. But as internal promotion is the primary means of finding managerial talent, broader coverage might be expected – at the very least to include *all* managerial levels. We shall return to this topic again when we consider equal opportunity issues relating to women.

Though appraisal schemes are used widely as a means of assessing potential, the validity of the assessments is rarely tested. If one assumed that the ratings – whether they be of performance or potential – had some degree of validity, they would represent a convenient summary allowing comparisons to be made between individuals – very useful for promotion decisions. But uncritical acceptance of the accuracy of ratings may be a mistake, as they are subject to various distorting influences. We discussed these earlier for performance ratings and the previous comments apply just as much to ratings of potential. In addition, it is not always clear *how* potential ratings are made; in other words what factors does the manager take into account in making the ratings. Presumably, past performance is the major consideration and it may be the only rational basis open to the manager. But jobs at higher levels may present different performance demands, thereby reducing the value of predictions based on past performance. Furthermore, the manager may have only a sketchy idea of job demands at higher levels – particularly above his own or in different functions – and this may make it difficult to extrapolate from the past to the future. Requiring the manager's boss to comment on or moderate the rating(s) is thought to be helpful, but this will be so only to the extent that the manager's boss has first-hand knowledge of the appraisee's performance.

Providing managers with some guidance on the criteria for advancement to the next level may help them in making their assessments, but many organizations simply fail to do this and even when they do so, it is not done very well.[13] Furthermore, training in the assessment of potential is likely to be deficient. Careful training, akin to that provided for assessment centre assessors, is perhaps what is required. And there are still other distorting influences. As organizations contract and opportunities for promotion diminish, some managers may give the appraisee a somewhat higher rating than is merited in order to give the individual a better chance of being considered for promotion. And some managers may feel that it will reflect well on them if they give 'good' promotion/potential ratings to their appraisees.

Though appraisal schemes are very widely used as a means of assessing promotability/potential, they rarely stand alone; most organizations use at least one other method, often at the time a promotion decision has to be made. For example, a confidential report may be obtained from the line manager. This may be useful if the appraisal report is perhaps several months old. However, such an arrangement may, in effect, be a dual reporting system in which the manager uses the confidential report to give a more critical assessment which is not disclosed to the individual.

Of the other assessment devices, the interview is the most popular. Unfortunately, there is abundant evidence[14] to show that interviews are notoriously unreliable for predicting job performance. As for formal appraisals and supplementary confidential reports, there is little evidence one way or the other as to their validity in this respect, but, from what we have said already about the former, their worth must be highly suspect. The merits of combining such methods therefore seem rather hard to discern unless they have been astonishingly well developed, implemented, and integrated! There are more rigorous methods and we shall say something about these in the next chapter.

The principal means of identifying training and development needs appears to be the appraisal scheme. The training and development section of the report form ought to have a broad purpose, and contain specific comments on what is required: it is not sufficient to say something like 'needs to attend a management training course' because such a statement is far too vague. Appraisal information which is of poor quality, and of insufficient quantity, reduces the ability of the training function to respond appropriately.[15]

It is not only at appraisal time that the manager might be expected to comment on training, and nor should the manager be the only person in the line to have a say – after all, the person believed to be in need of training may have views about the matter. In fact, however, many individuals do not have their training needs assessed before they attend a course and they often are not involved in decisions about off-the-job development.[6] Some of the difficulties in this area may be because of lack of skill in identifying needs – on the parts of both manager and subordinate. And, because of lack of information about training and development opportunities, ways of meeting the needs may be poorly specified. For example, managers may have insufficient information about the content of training courses or they may not know what courses exist. Hopefully, they will know where to go to get such information and appropriate help, but even this may be in doubt, as Ashton and Taylor[17] found that many managers were uncertain of the help that they might get from personnel and training specialists, particularly with regard to individual cases.

As well as having a responsibility for identifying training and development needs, managers may also have some responsibility for meeting such needs. Consider, for example, the use of appraisal schemes which have as one of their aims improving performance. For this aim to be fulfilled it might be argued that individuals need feedback on performance. The feedback might come from the appraisee being shown the completed report form and thereby seeing what has been written by the manager. In addition there is likely to be an appraisal interview, and this is another vehicle for giving feedback. But whatever the medium the feedback must be specific in terms of job performance and work behaviour if it is to have any developmental value.

Quite apart from providing feedback through the appraisal scheme, the line manager can influence individual development in other ways: direct action through on-the-job coaching, special assignments, delegation, job redesign. But even though there is much that the manager can do, there are pressures to make sure that the work gets done and these may act as a deterrent against spending time on training and development. These same pressures may make the manager reluctant to release people for training activities or to let good people move to other jobs, even though to do so may be to their (and the organization's) longer-term benefit.

The responsibilities of individuals themselves might be thought to be no less important, but in actual practice it seems that the individual often tends to be seen as a passive party. Self-appraisal is uncommon, training needs are probably not identified before attending a course, and the individual is often not consulted about training decisions. There are some signs of change as evidenced by the growth of interest in self-development that has taken place.

How come we find ourselves here?

Taken overall, the typical appraisal system operated by organizations in this country has some notable merits: it is present- and future-orientated; reasonably comprehensive without being over-cumbersome; job-related for the most part; provides some basis for making comparisons between people; is open and has a degree of flexibility in its content; and is not linked very closely with financial rewards. On the negative side: it reflects the views of a few senior managers and personnel specialists rather than the needs and notions of the people (appraisers and appraisees) who will be on the receiving end; the training given is inadequate – especially in relation to interviewing skills; by seeking to get the advantages of both results-orientated and rating methods it gets the disadvantages of both as well; whatever the dubious value of including an overall rating for comparability purposes, it is hard to disagree with Fournies'[18] view that such a rating 'provides no functional basis for training and development and brings management appraisal back to the level of grading eggs'; the degree of appraisee participation might best be described as limited; its capacity as a feedback process for subordinates is open to question; the use made of the appraisal data subsequently is not all that it should be; the various aims of the whole exercise may be antagonistic to one another;

whole groups of staff are excluded from the scheme for no obvious good reason.

Given all this, it is not surprising to find that many organizations doubt the effectiveness of their appraisal scheme. For example, in a survey of management development practices in British companies, Attwood[19] found that 41 per cent (37) of the responding organizations said that their appraisal scheme could be better or that it was ineffective; and that may represent an unduly optimistic viewpoint. So there are grounds for doubting the effectiveness of other management development activities which have a link with appraisal. Though a link may exist in theory, in actual practice it may be weak or non-existent, and where that is the case frustration develops and appraisal is seen in an unfavourable light.[20] This is merely one illustration of the more general problem of the interrelationships between career development systems.

A similar general problem is that there is often a discrepancy between what is supposed to happen and what actually happens. A particular instance concerns the assessment of training needs. More broadly, the intent of the management development objectives to meet individual needs may not be borne out in practice – there is a clear bias towards organization needs. Other deficiencies of management development are as for appraisal: the apparent exclusion of some management levels; the low level of participation in training decisions by prospective trainees; the low level of consultation with consumers during the development of the system. In fact, the typical appraisal and development system is just what one might expect it to be – a compromise between competing aims, interests and pressures. It is not very hard to find out how this has come about. We have already seen in the previous chapter how changes in social and organizational climates have had an influence on appraisal practices, and the way both practical experience and the findings of research have caused people to take a long, hard look at rating scales, at the various aims appraisals try to fulfil, and so on. Legislation and union pressures have had a bearing too. So while the *basic* aim of appraisal has remained much the same – motivating staff to improve performance – organizations have faced a series of conflicting ideas on how to go about achieving it. The deficiencies of the rating method and of personality-orientated appraisal, including the reluctance of appraisers to criticize and the alleged demotivating effects if they do, have led to the adoption of the objective-setting approach. This has had a further boost from the implications of equal opportunities legislation that appraisal schemes must be demonstrably job-related. But organizations still have to make comparisons between people for various purposes, so some use of ratings persists. The move towards openness in appraisal has been a reflection of a vague feeling that this is in keeping with the times and contemporary attitudes, as well as being partly a result of union pressures in some cases. But the danger of lack of frankness as a consequence of open appraisal has stopped all but the boldest from going all the way on disclosure; hence the assessment of potential usually remains closed.

There is compromise, too, in the resourcing of performance appraisal and career development. The need is recognized, and some time and expense go into training and running the system. But this always takes place against the background of what most people in the organization see as the top priority – the day-to-day work pressures that have to be coped with, the 'sharp end' of the operation. The result is that the system usually does not have adequate resources, the training is superficial, the monitoring inefficient and the evaluation non-existent. But the whole thing is still supposed to work anyway – or, at least, this is the view of many organizations. So, while one can appreciate the reasons for the way the typical present day system has evolved, the compromise achieved is not entirely a happy one. In performance appraisal, as in many other things, what one tends to get out depends on what one puts in. The typical appraisal system is trying to achieve too much with too little; the wonder is that it manages to do as well as it does.

Summary

Using the device of an 'Identikit', this chapter described the typical British appraisal system and approach to career development. Weaknesses of typical practices include inadequate training in appraisal interviewing skills and in assessing potential, the exclusion of certain categories of employees, limited opportunities for employee participation and involvement, and a multiplicity of potentially conflicting objectives which are over-biased towards organizational ends. On the positive side, today's typical appraisal practices are job-related for the most part and are both present- and future-orientated, having a reasonable amount of flexibility in their content. They do provide some basis for making comparisons between employees, and they are moving towards a degree of openness. Whilst the use made of appraisal data is not always as beneficial as it might be, the typical system at least has the merit of not being too closely tied to financial rewards. The links between appraisal and other career development systems are generally inadequate. The system an organization ends up with is inevitably the result of a compromise between a variety of competing aims, interests and pressures.

References

1   D. Gill, B. Ungerson and M. Thakur, *Performance Appraisal in Perspective*, IPM Information Report No. 14 (Institute of Personnel Management 1973).
    D. Gill, *Appraising Performance: Present Trends and the Next Decade*, IPM Information Report No. 25 (Institute of Personnel Management 1977).
    E. Anstey, C. Fletcher and J. Walker, *Staff Appraisal and Development* (George Allen and Unwin 1976).
    J. Walker, C. Fletcher, R. Williams and K. Taylor, 'Performance Appraisal: an Open or Shut Case?', *Personnel Review*, **6** (1977), pp. 38–42.
    P. Long, *Performance Appraisal Revisited* (Institute of Personnel Management 1986).
    S. Bevan, M. Thompson and W. Hirsh, *Performance Management in the UK* (Institute of Manpower Studies 1991).
2   D. McGregor, 'An uneasy look at performance appraisal', *Harvard Business Review*, **35** (1957), pp. 89–94.
    H.H. Meyer, E. Kay and J.R.P. French, Jr., 'Split roles in performance appraisal', *Harvard Business Review*, **43** (1965), pp. 123–9
    R.J. Burke, 'Why performance appraisal systems fail,' *Personnel Administration* (May/June 1972), pp. 32–40
    D. Pym, 'The politics and rituals of appraisals', *Occupational Psychology*, **47** (1973) pp. 231–5.
3   N.R.F. Maier, 'Three types of appraisal interview', *Personnel* (March/April 1958), pp. 27–40.
4   Anstey *et al., Staff Appraisal and Development.*
5   R.F. Holdsworth, *Identifying Managerial Potential*, BIM Management Survey Report, **27** (British Institute of Management 1975)
6   D.W. Brinkerhoff and R.M. Kanter, 'Appraising the performance of performance appraisal', *Sloane Management Review*, **21** (1980), pp. 3–15.
7   F.J. Landy and J.L. Farr, *The Measurement of Work Performance* (Academic Press 1983).
8   Gill, *Appraising Performance: Present Trends and the Next Decade.*
    Walker *et al.* 'Performance Appraisal: an Open or Shut Case?'
9   R. Wraith, *Appraisal for Staff Development: A Public Sector Study* (Royal Institute of Public Administration 1975).
10 Anstey *et al., Staff Appraisal and Development.*
11 B.W. Denning, D.E. Hussy and P.G. Newman, *Management Development – what to look for* (Harbridge House Europe 1978).
    L.T. Attwood, 'Management development in British companies,' *Journal of European Industrial Training*, **3** (1979).
    M. Koudra, *Management Training – practice and attitudes*, Management Survey Report No. 24, (British Institute of Management 1975).
    Gill, *Appraising Performance: Present Trends and the Next Decade.*
    Holdsworth, *Identifying Managerial Potential.*
12 Denning *et al., Management Development – what to look for*
    Attwood, 'Management development in British companies'.
13 A. Stewart and V. Stewart, *The Assessment of Potential – A survey of current practice* (The Institute of Manpower Studies 1976).
14 P. Herriot, 'The selection interview', in P. Herriot (ed.), *Assessment and Selection in Organizations* (Wiley 1989).
15 D. Ashton and P. Taylor, 'Current practices and issues in management appraisal', *Management Decision*, **12** (1974).
16 Koudra, *Management Training – practice and attitudes.*
17 Ashton and Taylor, 'Current practices and issues in management appraisal'.

18   F.F. Fournies, *Management Performance Appraisal – A National Study*, (F.F. Fournies Associates 1973).
19   Attwood, 'Management development in British companies'.
20   D. Ashton and M. Easterby-Smith, *Management Development in the Organisation: Analysis and Action*, (Macmillan 1979).

Case Study 1

An organization with an appraisal system which is typical in many of its features, but which has been put into operation with care and commitment.

This is a large commercial concern which has annual appraisals covering most of the 3500 management and supervisory staff. Employees below these levels are only appraised when recommended for promotion. The appraisers are given two days' training, including practice interviews. The normal pattern is for 'father' to do the appraisal after consulting 'grandfather' (who later countersigns the report).

There is an element of appraisee participation through the completion of the appraisal preparation form beforehand. The performance appraisal form itself (which is short – covering strengths and weaknesses, performance characteristics and overall ratings, and action plans) is usually filled in by the manager during or after the interview, though some preliminary notes and markings will have been made in advance. In the appraisal interview, the manager usually goes through the subordinate's comments on the preparation form and discussion takes place on any major discrepancies between the points of view of the two parties. Afterwards, the appraisal form is completed and the subordinate reads and signs it. During the interview another form is given to the appraisee to take away and fill in during the next few days. This is an 'Agreed targets' form, and, as its name implies, it lists the targets for the next year, leaving space for written comments when progress towards them is reviewed. This form and its contents are discussed with the appraiser about a week after the performance appraisal interview; the appraiser can modify the targets if he sees fit.

The annual review of potential is done some time after the appraisal and is closed. The company feels that current performance is a good guide to future potential, and the appraisal form plays a part in the promotion procedure – but not as much weight is attached to it in this context as the company would like. Assessment centre techniques are being increasingly used by this organization, which is generally speaking one of the more advanced in its approach to appraisal and development. A final point is that the company consulted a large proportion of its senior management in the process of developing its present appraisal system.

Case Study 2

An appraisal scheme that illustrates many of the problems and trends in the field over recent years.

This is a public sector organization employing something over 4000 people in and around London. The managers involved had little experience of appraisal when the new system was implemented in the late 1960s and early 1970s. The aims of appraisal were chiefly to provide feedback and improve performance, and to establish a way of comparing individuals for the purpose of promotion.

The appraisal form was too long (eight sides) and was not based on any job analysis. It was in fact drawn up by a committee, and looked like it. The main sections included a job description, a free-written assessment of how well the activities in the job description had been performed, numerous ratings (of performance characteristics, overall performance, fitness for promotion, and long-term potential), and further free-written sections by 'father' and 'grandfather'. The former completed the report and the latter held an appraisal interview before adding comments and signing the form. The same form was used for first level supervisors and senior managers – so uniformity and comparability were put before job relevance.

The appraisal scheme was introduced very carefully, with good training for the appraisers in both report completion and appraisal interviewing (around three to four days of training in all). The first people involved were top management and it was introduced at progressively lower levels afterwards. As this was a 'closed' system, particular attention was given to the appraisal interview and its handling. The interviewer was intended to convey the gist of the report without disclosing the exact contents. Appraisee self-review was encouraged and an interview preparation form was provided to facilitate this.

Trade union pressure for an open appraisal scheme eventually led the organization to shift in this direction; but having put a lot into implementing the original scheme, there was little enthusiasm for making wholesale changes. The result was that a degree of openness was grafted on to the existing process – the appraiser was permitted to disclose some previously closed elements of the appraisal if the appraisee requested. This leaves 'grandfather' the task of showing the appraisee the rating(s) given by 'father', a potentially very difficult situation. But how these new procedures are working out in practice has not been monitored systematically.

Associated with the appraisal systems was a new career development package which offered career interviews with central personnel staff at regular intervals, the aim being to obtain a better fit between the needs of individuals and those of the organization. In the late 1970s this system began to falter as successive Government 'cuts' forced reductions in staffing levels.

Case Study 3

An appraisal system that failed, and how they got it right the second time around

This case study is about the development of two performance evaluation systems for managers in New York City. A report on revisions to the city's charter argued the case for a new performance evaluation system to help overcome what was seen as a wide range of management problems – for example, deteriorating services, low productivity – by encouraging managerial accountability and rewarding outstanding performance. In addition, the existing system seemed to have been all but discredited; it was suffering from typical rating errors and managers generally found it difficult to use.

Research staff from the city's Personnel Department set about the task of developing a new system which was to be used for a wide range of purposes: ' ... to identify strengths, deficiencies, and development needs; assess potential for re-assignment and advancement; award pay increases; and make decisions as to retention or removal during the probationary periods.'

The first system to be developed was called the Managerial Performance Appraisal System (MPAS). It was a comprehensive, results-orientated approach with a strong management-by-objectives flavour. Goals would be set at the top-most level and these would govern the establishment of goals at successively lower levels, thereby ensuring that individual managers' tasks were in line with overall objectives. Discussions between each manager and his or her supervisor would focus on:

- The manager's key responsibilities, that is, why the position exists.

- Expected results, that is, objectives.

- Performance standards, that is, the basis for the evaluation of actual achievements.

- Action plans, that is, work planning and the statement of steps against which progress might be measured.

The outcome of the discussion was to be recorded on a specially designed form. Quarterly progress meetings were expected, in addition to informal discussions between manager and supervisor, to review progress and revise results and standards, if appropriate. Assessment of performance was to be in terms of five categories, ranging from outstanding to unsatisfactory. The definition of each category was in terms of 'the extent to which expected results were exceeded, attained, or not attained', including other considerations such as goal difficulty and importance, and extenuating circumstances. As well as rating performance the assessment was expected to cover such things as strengths and deficiencies in performance, personal development plans, and salary and career development recommendations.

As MPAS was to be the cornerstone for other activities it was decided to install the system quickly (within one year), although the research team who designed the system had argued for a number of years. The implementation phase included training and briefings for top level executives and training for all other managers. The initial plans for top executive training were found to be unrealistic – the executives would not devote time to attend a seven-session course – and a revised two-session programme therefore had to be devised. Quite apart from this, lack of commitment was evident on the part of the city's political leadership and this contributed to lower level managers attaching little credence to the system. Added to this, managers saw no tangible benefits in the system; many refused to adopt the participatory style required by the new system; there was resistance to planning and the quantification of standards; and the extra paperwork was disliked.

It therefore rapidly became apparent that the new system was not being taken seriously. It was seen as being too complex, too demanding of managers' time, and it interfered with operations. The system was reviewed by a private citizens group at the request of the Mayor's office. 'The group recommended that the system be streamlined to focus only on essential elements and to interfere as little as possible with ongoing operations.'

The revised system

Taking into account comments received from all quarters, the research team began to rethink the appraisal system. They came up with a much simpler scheme, having fewer purposes, called the Managerial Performance Evaluation (MPE) system. The emphasis in this system was on salary review, but it was designed in such a way as to allow other purposes to be included later. At the heart of the system's documentation was a one-page form. The philosophy was still results-orientated, but operated in a somewhat simpler fashion: the discussion, between manager and supervisor of key responsibilities and performance expectations remained, but with less emphasis on quantification. Expectations could be set out in other terms – timeliness, quality, behaviour – if appropriate.

The assessment, too, was simplified: there was to be a narrative assessment on actual performance, and a rating for each key responsibility. An overall rating was required to take into account the key responsibility ratings and any other significant performance events. There were three rating levels: outstanding, satisfactory, unsatisfactory.

Mayoral support was received, the system was ordered to be implemented and monitored, and the payment of salary increases was to be tied closely to the performance evaluation. Limited training was offered, but supported by a guidance booklet. The strong mayoral support helped acceptance of the revised system and managers found MPE easier to operate than MPAS had been. There were still a few problems, though. The definition of the rating category 'satisfactory' caused some concern. It was intended to reflect fully acceptable or good performance but was seen by some as implying only marginal performance. There was a fear that too many 'outstanding' ratings would be given because of the possible stigma attaching to 'satisfactory'. Doubts were expressed as to whether pay increases would actually be linked to performance. The consequences of the performance ratings had been explained (for example, larger than average increases would be paid to outstanding managers), but there was uncertainty about the actual size of increase which would be associated with 'outstanding' or 'satisfactory' performance. A related difficulty was that of managers not giving 'unsatisfactory' ratings where performance merited it because this would result in the non-payment of an increase. Despite these difficulties, an audit of the early stages of the revised system showed that MPE had got off to a promising start: the large majority of managers had been able to define measurable performance expectations; progress in meeting them was being measured; and the appropriateness of performance expectations was being assessed in the light of initial experience with the system.

Deriving from the experience of devising these two systems, the research teams identified a number of guidelines relevant to the installation of performance appraisal programmes.

1   Get top level support.
2   Is the system in keeping with the goals of the top level political leaders?
3   Systematically monitor and follow-up the programme.
4   Keep the system simple.
5   The system must have built-in tangible rewards and incentives.
6   Existing practices and preferences should be utilized as much as possible.
7   Sufficient time should be allowed for the system to take hold.
8   The system should interfere with or disrupt existing management practices and styles as little as possible.

4
The outer limits

In Chapter 3 we described typical performance appraisal and career development practices, but made only passing references to some of the less commonly used approaches. We redress this imbalance here. The chapter has three main sections. First, we consider methods of assessing past performance which are little used. Second, we look at methods of assessing potential. And finally we explore individual participation in appraisal and career development.

Methods of assessing past performance

Apart from the results-orientated and rating approaches described already, other approaches to assessing performance include personality ratings, narrative or essay methods and critical incidents. There have also been some new developments in rating scale formats. These methods may well be used in combination with each other, and in combination with the more popular approaches.

Personality ratings
Appraisal forms which include personality ratings usually present for assessment a list of personal qualities or characteristics, such as judgement, loyalty, initiative – that is, to what degree does the individual possess this trait? On some forms the characteristics are defined.

Personality ratings suffer from the disadvantages of the rating method as described in Chapter 2 – ambiguity, subjectivity, rater errors, etc. The upshot of all these disadvantages is to limit the usefulness of the information which is generated. For example, there tends to be a lack of discrimination amongst ratings of different dimensions (or characteristics), and it becomes difficult to discriminate amongst the individuals who have been rated. And the ratings themselves – particularly those of personality – have little development value for the individual. Given all these inherent weaknesses, the supposed advantages of personality ratings must surely be illusory. Yet, surprisingly, ratings of personality traits saw something of a rise in popularity in the latter part of the 1970s as compared with the beginning of the decade.[1] It is difficult to account for this apparent increase: perhaps it is a reflection of the fact that, although extremely difficult to assess, personal qualities are nonetheless important for effective performance.

Narratives or essays

There are two approaches here. One is where the appraiser simply writes a 'pen-picture' of the individual and his or her performance during the year. The second provides headings of some kind in order to guide the appraiser in what to write.

The main advantages of essays are that they allow appraisers to use their own words and to concentrate on what they see as the most significant aspects of appraisees and their job performance; and a well-written narrative can provide a vivid pen-picture of the person being appraised. But, against these points, a well-written narrative relies on the memory and conscientiousness of the appraiser and on his or her literary skills.

Significant aspects of performance may be omitted. As with other assessment methods, the narrative may reflect the appraiser's personal biases. It is difficult to compare narratives from one individual to another, hence limiting their value for administrative purposes.

Critical incidents

This approach is described by Warr and Bird[2] in the context of identifying supervisory training needs, but it may also be used in various ways in the assessment of performance. One way might be as follows. At the end of the year the appraiser is instructed, on the appraisal form, to describe two incidents: one in which the appraisee had been especially effective, and the other an incident which was performed in a particularly ineffective way. To aid completion, guidelines might be given – who else was involved? were there other similar incidents? what were the consequences? etc.

Used in this way, the critical incident technique can be looked on as a variant of the essay approaches just described. As such, it has much the same advantages and disadvantages as do essays. Potentially it offers scope for a more balanced assessment – by asking for effective and ineffective incidents – but this concentration on the extremes does at the same time ignore a large part of the appraisee's performance. The approach also assumes, of course, that critical incidents can be found in an appraisee's performance. The usefulness of the approach is increased when it is applied throughout the year, rather than just at the end. In one American organization, for example, supervisors record incidents which meet one or the other of two criteria:

- The incident has direct impact on the meeting of job responsibilities and work quality and quantity.

- The incident produces a work performance situation that would normally be discussed immediately with the employee.

Incidents are recorded when they occur (for example, the date, nature of the incident) and the supervisor is expected to give feedback on the performance at the time, whether it be to show appreciation of good performance or to give counselling to help with poor performance. The record of incidents through the year forms the basis of the end-of-year appraisal report. The organization provides guidance on how to interpret patterns or trends in the occurrence of incidents, as shown in Example 4.1

Example 4.1 *Guidelines on interpreting critical incidents*

The number of incidents recorded will vary from employee to employee. Patterns or trends in the occurrence of 'incidents' may be interpreted in the light of the following guidelines:

- Poor performance 'incidents' grouped in a short time period may indicate personal or other outside reasons for their occurrence.

- Poor performance 'incidents' spread throughout the period may indicate that the employee is poorly trained, does not have sufficient experience or background, is not properly motivated, or does not understand the job expected of him or her.

- Poor performance 'incidents' at the beginning of the appraisal period which decrease in frequency towards the end or become good performance 'incidents' may show that the employee is improving in job expertise and is progressing well.

- Good performance 'incidents', either grouped or distributed throughout the appraisal period, may indicate better than expected job performance by the employee.

- No 'incidents' or only a few scattered throughout the appraisal period may show generally that the expected job is being performed, or that the supervisor has not been closely aware of an employee's performance.

The incidents are reviewed in relation to the employee's responsibilities. For example, a number of repeat 'incidents' under one job responsibility shows a potentially serious situation if they are poor performance 'incidents'. It may mean that the individual continues to make the same mistakes over and over. This is especially serious if the situation has been discussed with the employee.

A particular advantage of using the critical incidents approach in this way is that it avoids the danger of the 'recency effect', that is, appraisers basing their appraisals on what happened in the few weeks or months before the report was written. The approach is useful for developmental purposes; not only is there an encouragement to provide appropriate feedback at the time of the incident, there is also a record to be drawn upon for the appraisal interview. The major disadvantage, perhaps, is that comparability, of one appraisee with another, suffers.

Newer rating methods

The difficulties with conventional rating scales have led practitioners to consider new types. One which has been reported quite often in the literature – particularly North American – is the *Behaviourally Anchored Rating Scale* (or BARS). These scales sometimes are called *Behavioural Expectation Scales* (BES) and this term gives a clue to the nature of the scale. An example is provided in Figure 1. As can be seen, the essence of the scale is a focus on behaviour – what the person actually does to demonstrate a particular aspect of work performance.

BARS are difficult and time-consuming to develop because of the fivefold procedure involved:

1   Specific examples of effective and ineffective job performance are obtained from people ('experts') who are knowledgeable about the job in question. The critical incidents approach or repertory grid can be useful here.

2   The examples are grouped into performance dimensions by the panel of 'experts'.

3   A second group of 'experts' reallocates the examples generated in step 1 to the dimensions identified in step 2. The purpose of this step is to eliminate ambiguous examples of behaviour and ensure, as far as possible, that the dimensions are independent of each other.

4   For each dimension the performance examples are rated (by the second group) on, say, a seven-point scale ranging from most effective to least effective, or outstanding performance to poor performance. Examples which show wide variability in their ratings are discarded.

5   Finally, the scales are set out – one for each performance dimension – by *anchoring* each scale point with a description of the *expected* behaviour at that level of effectiveness.

The number of dimensions to be rated will vary according to the nature of the job – between six and nine seems quite common. For example, one British study[3] generated seven: supervision of operators, scheduling and planning, technical troubleshooting, handling men, communications, administrative problems of wiring wire, and dealing with other departments. This high degree of job relatedness of BARS is

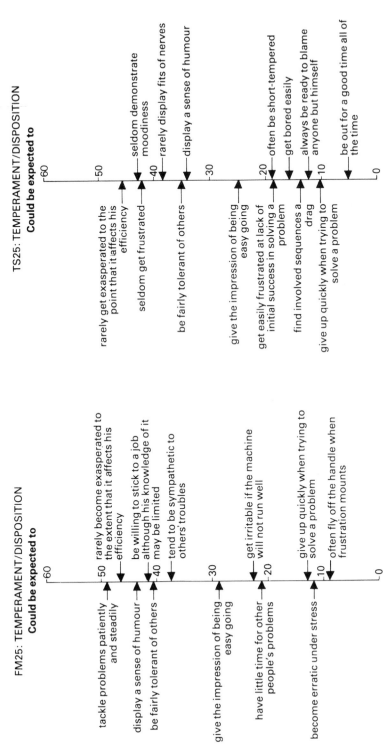

Figure 1 *Examples of behaviourally anchored rating scales*
These examples illustrate how a personality characteristic can be defined in behavioural terms. They also show how the position of the rate influences the way in which the characteristics' anchors are defined (FM = Floor Manager TS = Technical Supervisor). From C.T. Bailey, *The Measurement of Job Performance* (Gower Press 1983)

clearly a considerable advantage, but, on the other hand, the development process is time-consuming and costly, and to produce separate appraisal forms for every job may not be feasible. However, some research[4] has shown that BARS can be developed to cut across jobs – in this particular case from manual jobs such as floor sweepers and dishwashers, through clerks, and on to technical and professional positions such as laboratory technicians and social workers. Ten dimensions of performance were identified: interpersonal relationships, organizing and planning, reactions to problems, reliability, communicating, adaptability, growth (in the sense of increasing knowledge, understanding and skills), productivity, quality of work, and teaching.

BARS have several advantages. The anchors are behavioural in nature and they reflect the language actually used by appraisers. This may help to reduce ambiguity. Appraisers are involved in the development of the scales and this may help to increase commitment to the end product. The behavioural nature of the scales adds to their value for developmental purposes, particularly if appraisers have to give examples of incidents or performance which support their ratings. Development of the scales is rigorous, although this is at the same time a potential disadvantage because of the cost involved. However, by taking a broader view of the development process – in effect, seeing it as a job analysis exercise – the cost perhaps becomes more acceptable. The development process generates a large amount of data at the outset, but much of the information is lost at successive steps in the process of producing rating scales. The data may, however, be put to other purposes – for example, to help design training courses, and in developing criteria for promotion procedures.

Disadvantages of BARS involve their usage by appraisers. For example, one problem which has been encountered is that appraisers are sometimes unable to decide what dimension of performance is demonstrated by a particular instance of behaviour. Following on from this, even when the appropriate performance dimensions have been identified, it can be difficult to decide what level of performance – according to the scale – compares with the displayed instance. In short, raters are not always able to match the job behaviour they observe with the anchors on the rating scales. Furthermore, the research evidence shows mixed results with BARS, and their early promise as being technically superior to conventional scales has not always been borne out. Viewed narrowly as an evaluation device, therefore, BARS seem not to have much going for them. But by taking a broader view of the value of the development process as a whole the case for them becomes much stronger.

There are other developments in behavioural rating, one example being the Behavioural Observation Scale (BOS)[5] which is similar to the

Example 4.2   *Hypothetical illustration of a behavioural observation scale*

Leadership/staff supervision

1 Provides help, training and guidance so that employees can improve their performance.

   Almost never   5   4   3   2   1   Almost always

2 Explains to staff exactly what is expected of them – staff know their job responsibilities.

   Almost never   5   4   3   2   1   Almost always

3 Gets involved in subordinates' work only to check it

   Almost never   5   4   3   2   1   Almost always

4 Consult staff for their ideas on ways of making their jobs better.

   Almost never   5   4   3   2   1   Almost always

5 Praises staff for things they do well.

   Almost never   5   4   3   2   1   Almost always

6 Passes important information to subordinates.

   Almost never   5   4   3   2   1   Almost always

The number of behavioural statements to be rated for any one dimension will be determined through the job analysis used to identify the key dimensions of performance and behavioural statements.

performance questionnaires described by Stewart and Stewart.[6] A hypothetical illustration is provided in Example 4.2. As with BARS, the BOS development procedure, though rather different (see Latham and Wexley[7]) is time-consuming but potentially advantageous from the broader point of view. The end result is the identification of a number of dimensions of performance, for each of which there is a number of behavioural statements. Subordinates are rated according to the extent to which they demonstrate these behaviours. A score for each performance dimension can be obtained simply by adding together the assigned ratings; an overall performance score can be obtained in the same way. The advantages and disadvantages of BOS are comparable to those of BARS. BOS, however, have not been subject to the same degree of empirical study as have other rating formats, and some uncertainty must therefore remain over their technical properties.

Methods of assessing potential

Appraisal systems

In the previous chapter we showed that the appraisal system is a commonly used tool for assessing promotability/potential. The assessment most often is a part of the appraisal form which is closed to the appraisee. Some organizations, however, use a separate form to record potential assessments. Sometimes this is done so as to avoid the conflicts of assessing past performance and future potential in one and the same scheme. Often, though, it is because organizations want to keep secret their potential assessments. This therefore raises the question of openness in appraisal, an issue to which we shall return more fully later on. For the present, though, it is sufficient to note that a separate potential assessment on a closed form is believed to be more accurate than assessments made in other appraisal circumstances. If this is true, then it clearly is an advantage. A disadvantage of a separate system is that it may result in extra paperwork and added complexity, which may not be acceptable to the line managers expected to make the assessments.

Psychological tests

Assessment methods like appraisals are based on the principle that past behaviour can predict future behaviour. This is true up to a point, but assessments made on this basis are subject to error, as our earlier discussions of the assessment of past performance have shown. However, there are other assessment methods which can predict future performance: these include psychological tests and simulation exercises. It is difficult to gauge precisely the extent to which such methods are used but various surveys[8] indicate that their usage has increased.

Various kinds of psychological tests are used, either singly or in combination with each other or with other methods. Types of test include general intelligence tests, tests of special aptitudes, tests of knowledge or achievements, and personality questionnaires. Evidence about the validity of psychological tests is, it must be admitted, equivocal; it seems clear that tests can make a potentially valuable contribution to assessments, but simply to take a seemingly appropriate test (or tests) off-the-peg and hope for the best is not enough. The tests have to be tailored to meet the particular requirement of the jobs concerned; in other words, the tests must be job-related. This requires job analysis and validation studies.[9]

Assessment Centres (ACs)

Job analysis and validation studies are also required for assessment centres to be used effectively. ACs often incorporate psychological tests along with simulations such as group discussions, in-tray exercises, business or management exercises, and interviews. As well as being multi-method, other characteristics of ACs are that they use several assessors (usually senior managers specially trained in assessment skills) and they assess several dimensions of performance required in the higher level positions.

Traditionally, the main purpose of assessment centres has been to contribute to management decisions about people – usually the assessment of management skills and potential as a basis for promotion decisions. ACs are better at predicting future performance than are judgements made by unskilled managers, and it is the combination of techniques which contributes to their apparent superiority over other approaches. ACs are undeniably expensive to set up, but even so there may be circumstances in which their use would be particularly appropriate. This is likely to be where relatively little is known about people, especially about their managerial abilities; this may be true of short-service employees or specialists of various kinds who may not have had the opportunity to demonstrate management ability. We shall come back to ACs later, but we conclude this section by looking at some illustrations of how they are used – see Examples 4.3 and 4.4.

Individual participation in appraisal and career development

Appraisee participation in appraisal

Whilst organizations typically recognize that appraisers have a major role in the operation of appraisal schemes, a much smaller part tends to be played by the appraisee. A few organizations do encourage appraisee self-appraisal in one way or another. One version is to give the appraisee a blank copy of the normal appraisal form to fill in. Self- appraisal of this kind is rare, and it has to be said that the research evidence on it may be off-putting as it suggests that self-ratings tend to be more lenient than those made by the appraisee's supervisors. This raises the question as to whether one set of ratings (for example, by supervisors) is necessarily more or less accurate than another (for example, by the appraisee or by peers); there is no simple answer to this question, but it is evident that job-holders tend to have different views of their performance from those of their managers. Perhaps appraisal schemes should therefore be designed so as to systematically incorporate these different viewpoints. An illustration of multiple appraisal is provided in Chapter 8.

Another kind of self-appraisal is preparation for the appraisal interview. Much more common than self-rating, this has increased in popularity considerably. The appraisee may be given a copy of the appraisal form to guide preparation or, more probably, there is a separate form especially designed for the purpose. The evidence in

Example 4.3   *The use of an assessment centre to select first-level supervisors*

The selection and training of first-level supervisors has been a long-standing problem for many organizations. In selecting such supervisors a commonplace practice has been to select the technically most competent workers, paying scant regard to their ability to manage the work of others. Training, and the subsequent treatment, of supervisors by higher levels of management has been lacking too and many first-level supervisors have difficulty in coping with their new role – they see themselves as being in the middle, not knowing whether they are still one of the staff or part of management. These difficulties are well documented and they are found in clerical as well as blue-collar settings; descriptions of possible solutions are rather less common, however.

One approach to the selection of first-level supervisors is to use the assessment centre: the Ford Motor Company provides an example. Ford developed an assessment centre to assess five groups of characteristics:

1   Decision-making – for example, judgement
2   Management – for example, leadership
3   Interpersonal capability – for example, persuasiveness
4   Motivation – for example, initiative
5   Character and practical skills – for example, flexibility, practical learning

The assessment centre programme, which lasts one day, comprises five exercises: a scheduling problem requiring the written presentation of two solutions for later justification at an interview; a committee exercise; a role-play of a supervisor conducting a counselling interview; an exercise playing the part of a foreman taking over a section with production difficulties which require diagnosis and solution; an exercise requiring recommendations responding to six different case studies.

A testing programme (basic reasoning, verbal and numerical skills) was used to screen out those unlikely to have a chance of succeeding at the assessment centre. The testing programme also identified those with potential to succeed but who might be in need of remedial training to enhance their numerical and literary skills.

Those applying for foremanship and management have generally been favourably disposed towards the assessment centre.

Example 4.4   *The use of an assessment centre at mid-level: 'IMPACT'*[10]

This assessment centre (AC) was run by Standard Telephone and Cables (STC) and was called 'IMPACT', an acronym for Identification of Management Potential And Counselling Techniques, so reflecting its twin objectives of:

1   Identifying potential for senior management work in the company

2   Establishing the individual's training and career development needs, to assist in developing the potential which has been identified.

The dimensions considered to be important for successful performance at executive level in STC were drawn up using the Repertory Grid technique on a group of senior managers, by asking them to suggest the qualities which differentiate successful from less successful executives in the company. The dimensions are defined in detail so that the assessors know exactly what is meant by each one. The participants' performance on these dimensions is assessed using a number of different exercises constructed to simulate executive level work as closely as possible. Psychometric test data are also collected. The assessors rate the various characteristics using an eight-point scale, comparing the performance of participants with that of managers currently at senior level. They also make notes on the behaviour they have observed to support their ratings. Figure 2 lists the dimensions and the exercises to which they are related. The decision as to which dimensions relate to which exercises was made on intuitive grounds.

Twelve participants and six assessors attend each AC. The exercises last for two days and on the third day an assessors' conference is held at which all the information from the exercises is brought together to enable the assessors to reach their conclusions. The members of the panel of twenty assessors are almost without exception executives in line and staff jobs in the company, representing a wide range of functions and divisions and including representatives of HQ Staff and Training Departments. All assessors have attended an intensive three-day training session during which they took part in the group exercises, sat some of the written tests and had extensive practice at observing and evaluating behaviour.

The participants are all middle and junior managers, usually nominated by their divisional managers and/or career planning specialists; they are not self-nominated. The feedback discussion on their performance in the AC takes place three to six weeks afterwards and is conducted by one of the assessors. Apart from the participant and the assessor, the former's general manager or someone from the personnel function also attends. Evaluation research indicates that this crucial part of the AC process is Perceived very favourably by the participants.

Dimensions	*Exercises* In-tray	Committee Pt 1 (Presentation)	Committee Pt 2 (Discussion)	Business decisions (1)	Business decisions (2–5)	Business decisions (6–8)	Presentation (business plan)	Letter-writing	Total
1. Analytical ability	★			★	★		★		4
2. Helicopter ability	★		★			★			3
3. Administrative ability	★			★	★		★		4
4. Business sense	★			★	★	★	★		5
5. Written communication	★							★	2
6. Oral communication		★	★				★		3
7. Perceptive listening			★	★					2
8. Vigour	★		★	★		★			4
9. Emotional adjustment		★	★		★		★		4
10. Social skill			★		★	★		★	4
11. Ascendancy		★	★		★	★	★		5
12. Flexibility			★		★	★			3
13. Relations with subordinates	★		★					★	3
Total	7	3	9	5	7	6	6	3	46

Figure 2 *Dimensions assessed in each exercise*

support of this kind of self-appraisal is encouraging as it tends to be associated with positive interview outcomes such as improvement in work performance.

Participation in career development

The increased interest in self-appraisal is one tangible demonstration of the more general increase in participation in career development which is evident from the greater use of a variety of self-development methods. We shall review approaches to involvement shortly, after we comment briefly on the nature of self-development.

Self-development and self-directed learning

Conceptual confusion surrounds the term self-development. In our sub-heading we refer to self-development and self-directed learning; we believe that the latter term is encompassed by the former, although the two are often used interchangeably. Whilst self-directed learning is a form of self-development, the latter has other meanings also. Burgoyne, Boydell, and Pedler,[11] for example, list ten possible interpretations of self-development. Some might be looked on as definitions of self-directed learning: for example, 'any learning which results from self-initiated action', 'the learner taking responsibility for decisions at all stages of the learning process', 'learning without a teacher or trainer', 'the responsibility for implementing or transferring learning gained in more formal settings'. Self-development perhaps implies something more, incorporating notions of self-actualization, psychological growth and increased personal competence.

A particular difficulty which complicates our understanding of self-development centres on the distinction between development *of* self and development *by* self. Added to this distinction is that between *goals* (implicit in development *of* self) and *process* (associated with development *by* self). Though it is important to bear these distinctions in mind, particularly with regard to self-directed learning, it is clear (as Pedler and Boydell[12] point out in their later work) that the *of* self and *by* self dichotomy is not a hard-and-fast one when applied to self-development. As they point out, 'development by-self implies an of-self dimension', although whether the obverse is true is less clear.

The important practical consideration for an organization wishing to employ one or more of the many self-development approaches is that it needs to have a clear view of what it means by self-development. There is not necessarily anything more or less right about the various interpretations which have been put forward, and an organization may adopt any one or several of them in combination. By this means, the organization should be better able to specify what end results it wishes to achieve, and the means by which it wishes to achieve them.

The trend towards the use of self-development approaches is particularly evident in the context of management development. See Example 4.5 for an illustration. This shift has come about partly because of the build-up of evidence casting doubt on the value of much of traditional management training. Quite apart from this, it is argued that self-development approaches are particularly appropriate to management. This is not to say, though, that self-development approaches are the exclusive preserve of management. For example, North American experience suggests that blue collar employees and clerical staff can benefit from career planning workshops just as much as managers and professionals do. Example 4.6, which describes a programme for women returning to work, is particularly relevant to this. More generally, we would make the point that career development is also not the sole preserve of managerial and professional employees. That much of our discussion, and many of our examples, relating to

---

Example 4.5   *An approach to management development which seeks to achieve personal learning integrated with practical organizational improvements*[13]

This insurance company's approach to management training arose out of a belief that much formal management development activity within organizations had little effect, largely because of three main reasons:

- The links between management development activities and organizational and personal objectives are weak.

- There is inadequate support to enable people to apply learning.

- Tutoring methods, while concentrating on knowledge and skill development, do not help to change attitudes or overcome blocks to personal or organizational changes.

Accordingly, a supervisory development programme was devised with three principal features:

- All of the managers concerned (not just the participants but those at more senior levels too) were interviewed to seek their views so that they were fully involved, and this helped to build up support for the programme.

- The participating managers were helped to develop clear goals for personal learning and for improvement and change in the job.

- The programme was designed to help meet these goals. For example, the workshops were integrated with the job by involving higher levels of management as trainers, and the content of the workshops was highly practical through the use of job problems brought up by the managers themselves.

The programme comprised three separate workshops run at intervals of two months. The first workshop concentrated on such skills as planning, organizing, controlling and time management. The second workshop focused more on interpersonal skills, such as leadership, communication, influencing. Other interpersonal skills, for example, coaching and feedback, featured in the third workshop, along with staff development.

Evaluation of the programme indicated that it had contributed to improved work organization, more effective working relationships and better communication. Some of the organizational changes had led to improvements in productivity, for example.

---

managers may imply otherwise, but this is simply a reflection of contemporary organizational practice. Whilst we appreciate that organizational reality is such that most efforts will be directed at managers, we shall none the less argue for the broader view.

Example 4.6 *Providing career development help for women wanting to return to work*[14]

In 1978 and 1979 experimental 'Wider Opportunities for Women' ('WOW') courses were offered and an evaluation of them was carried out. The broad aims of the 'WOW' courses were to:

1   give information on available opportunities for employment, training and further education

2   help women make informed, realistic occupational plans

3   help women to acquire the necessary confidence and skills to take the next step forward.

The courses, which were offered in both full-time and part-time versions, were designed primarily for women likely to enter unskilled or semi-skilled employment. A key feature of the courses is the opportunity for self-assessment based upon practical experience of job and training samples, particularly of jobs usually not regarded as 'women's work'. Thus, opportunities were offered to try, for example, motor vehicle maintenance, welding, radio and television repairs, carpentry, plumbing, and visits were made to, for example, day nurseries and nursery schools. The courses also included: talks from outside speakers, for example, about areas of employment, training opportunities and job applications; revision sessions, in mathematics and English; group discussions; and group and individual counselling.

The experimental courses were attended by fifty women (three fewer than originally enrolled). Most were aged between twenty-six and forty-five, married, with children still at school, with no educational qualifications, and with some past work experience.

There were three main ways in which the women felt they had been affected by the course: increased confidence, re-evaluation of present circumstances, and clarification of goals. Particular aspects of the course which were valued by participants included receiving information on jobs and training, being shown new possibilities for employment not previously considered, and opportunities for self-assessment.

Methods of involvement
Such is the wide range of methods of involving individuals in their development that we cannot hope to describe them all here. We shall be selective therefore and concentrate on those that we believe to be most in evidence: workbooks and workshops, counselling and assessment centres. A review of other approaches is to be found in Burgoyne and others.[15]

Workbooks   Several, of various kinds, exist, some of which have now been available for many years. For example, the Local Government

Training Board has produced a multi-part workbook called *Could You be a Better Manager?* [16] *A Manager's Guide to Self-Development* [17] is well-known, and a comparable workbook of this type is called *The Unblocked Manager*. [18] An in-company workbook has been developed by Esso, [19] and in the future there will be other examples of proprietary workbooks in the same way that management training exercises frequently are tailored to suit the particular organization's circumstances. All of these are home-grown products. Many North American materials [20] also exist, and they are well worth exploring by anyone wishing to use them for themselves or in an organization.

Workshops To pursue a workbook to its conclusion requires a high degree of motivation on the part of the individual concerned. The help and support of others are needed and workbooks typically advocate such encouragement. To all intents and purposes, help and support is built into career planning workshops. These kinds of workshops have been offered by a number of training organizations for the past few years, and they may be increasingly used in the future. By way of illustration, the design of one British workshop is described in Example 4.7.

The general approach followed in workshops is to cover self-analysis, identification of opportunities, goal-setting, and planning. Workbooks typically follow a similar kind of pattern; indeed workbooks, or similar self-study materials, often form the basis of workshops, perhaps supplemented by paper-and-pencil tests. The major feature, though, of workshops is the use of group exercises and discussions which allow the interchange of ideas and information, and which provide the needed supportive atmosphere. Workshops may incorporate personal counselling sessions. Another feature of workshops, and this is becoming increasingly true of workbooks and other methods, is that they are concerned with career planning in a broad sense. As our definition of career planning, we adopt that advocated in an American Society of Training and Development publication: [22]

> 'A deliberate process for (1) becoming aware of self, opportunities, constraints, choices, and consequences, and for (2) identifying career related goals, and for (3) programming of work, education, and related developmental experiences to provide the direction, timing, and sequence of steps to attain a specific career goal.'

Reading this definition it is not hard to understand why management may be fearful of making career planning help available to employees. Typical fears are that the provision of career planning facilities will lead to increased employee turnover and mobility within the organization (we shall argue later that organizations may wish to encourage more internal mobility), raised expectations, and overburdening of existing training and development facilities. In fact, North American practice [23] suggests that these dangers are more apparent than real. The sorts of benefits which have been reported by participants include the following:

- Participants seek to upgrade existing skills or acquire new ones to open up other areas of work.
- Some participants have made changes to their job duties but there has not been any large-scale job changing.
- Increased self-understanding, of values, interests, abilities and other personal characteristics.
- Greater sense of personal responsibility for career planning and development.
- Greater awareness of what can be controlled and of available opportunities.
- Greater awareness of what cannot be controlled, for example, the various personnel policies, organizational structures, and such like, which may act as constraints or barriers.
- Participants felt better able to join in discussions with their managers about jobs and careers, and participants felt the quality of such discussions to be improved.
- Participants felt better able to resolve concerns over job, career, and family.

On the whole, these reactions were endorsed by participants' managers. Managers particularly felt that the quality of discussions about jobs and careers had improved and this was especially true for those managers who had themselves undertaken some kind of career planning activity. Also, there is some suggestion from managers that they have noticed a positive change in subordinates' morale and attitudes to work.

The effect that career planning workshops have had on employee expectations is not altogether clear, though there is no evidence to support the management fear that expectations are increased. Indeed, if anything, employees come away with a more realistic appreciation of their present circumstances and future prospects. If this is the case then there is some support for the rationale underlying much career planning activity, namely:

> '... the primary assumption is that the process of clarifying their own goals and their expectations of future organizational requirements can aid individuals in making decisions about career development activities which are more realistically feasible than would be possible without that clarification. A corollary assumption is that the motivation to act will be greater because the plans are self-generated.[24]

These two assumptions have been only partly borne out by North American experience so far. It is also worth noting that the majority of

Example 4.7   *A career and life planning workshop*[21]

The design of the workshop was based upon behavioural science developments in the two fields of career development and interpersonal skills. Career development was defined broadly so as to encompass the non-work implications of work-related career development decisions; the term 'life-goals planning' was, in fact, used for the workshop. The workshop design emphasized self-directed and student-controlled learning so as to encourage a climate in which participants could take stock of their achievements so far, and give careful thought to the future directions of their lives and careers. The workshop was aimed at middle managers.

The workshop was structured by means of a standard package of materials for each participant and a daily timetable of events. On each day, apart from the first and last, the first part of each morning and afternoon was spent working in small syndicate groups. The rest of each morning and afternoon was spent in plenary sessions.

The standard set of materials, presented as a Participant's Manual, comprised a series of individual and group exercises. The purpose of the exercises was to help participants explore themselves first – who they were and what they had been doing with their lives – as a basis for establishing career and life goals. There was a common pattern to the way in which the exercises were completed. First, each individual would complete the exercise alone. Then, group members were invited to work together to share their individual results with other members of their syndicate group. When everyone in the group was satisfied that they had worked through the exercise thoroughly they moved on to the next one in the Manual.

the programmes on which the foregoing evidence is based are quite small-scale in their scope and many of them had not been running for very long prior to evaluation. British evidence about workshops likewise is sparse, and suffers from the deficiencies described in the previous paragraph. But there is reason to believe[25] that benefits such as increased confidence, clarification of goals, clearer sense of career direction and enhanced commitment, and improved planning and execution, certainly can be expected. What effects workshops have beyond these depends on a number of factors. For example, the design of the workshop, the needs of the participants, and the environment of the organization. This last is particularly important as benefits derived by individuals may be dissipated if they are not reinforced. For example, action plans which entail job changing (a significant outcome of one workshop[26]) may not be fulfilled if the structure of the organization does not encourage internal mobility. It is no use just tacking on individual career planning activities to the already existing

The sequence of exercises was designed so as to move from a broad exploration of achievements and disappointments in life, as a whole, to an assessment of personal strengths and current constraints. This personal assessment then led to the establishment of goals and directions for personal change.

The Manual, with its sequence of fairly structured tasks, was liked by the participants for the sense of direction and purpose that it provided. Within the group, participants were able to control the level of self-disclosure which gradually rose from a low level as a climate of trust developed. As well as being a receiver of help from others, each group member was a provider of similar help, for example, by clarifying values or checking perceptions.

This dual role of being giver and receiver raised several questions about interpersonal relationships which were dealt with in the plenary sessions. What happened in the plenary sessions depended upon what happened in the syndicate groups. The tutor leading the plenary session was able to introduce exercises designed to practise specific skills, to present a lecture or handout, to introduce discussion groups, to use self-assessment questionnaires, or to adopt some other device to suit the demands. But whatever was done was only done after negotiation and agreement in the plenary session. The sorts of interpersonal skills which were explored included giving and receiving feedback, trust building, and confrontation and conflict resolution.

Participants' self-reports suggest that many found the workshop to have been a significant personal experience and that it was more related to their real needs than the traditional type of management course.

career management programmes; to encourage employee participation in career decision-making and then provide no organizational support is simply a kind of 'buck passing'. Recent North American experience has pointed to the need for managements to ensure that the organizational climate will reinforce a participative approach to career development.

Counselling Broadly speaking, there are two main 'types' of counselling. On the one hand, theirs is *developmental* counselling, as illustrated in Example 4.8 where it is used to identify development needs. On the other hand, there is *crisis* counselling where the emphasis is on helping the individual cope with, say, being made redundant. It is tempting to suggest that there are probably more examples of crisis counselling in organizations than of developmental counselling. In truth, though, it is hard to make any kind of judgement of this kind, partly because there are no relevant surveys of practice and partly because there is no common view as to what passes for counselling.

We do not wish to engage here in a lengthy conceptional discussion of

Example 4.8   *Counselling the development of senior managers*[27]

This programme, though operating in a large group, applies to only a small number (about forty) of the organization's senior executives. The chosen approach, while based on a counselling interview with a development adviser, is intended to push responsibility for looking at development needs back on to the individual manager and his boss:

As a preliminary step, the manager is approached initially by his boss, and then is sent a written note by the adviser explaining the background to the programme and what will happen. The discussion, which takes place in the manager's own office, ranges over the manager's past experience, the content of his present job and skills and knowledge required for it, the manager's own perceptions of his strengths and areas for improvement, current and future development needs, career interests, and possible solutions to the identified needs. The length of the interview varies between one and a quarter and four hours, on average being about two hours. The interviews are confidential and nothing is passed to anyone else without the agreement of the manager. Thus, following the interview the adviser prepares a note which is agreed with the manager before it goes to the boss. Additional comments relating to possible solutions may be added by the adviser following further thought after the conclusion of the interview.

After the manager has approved it, the report is sent to his or her boss with the intention that the two should discuss it, with the adviser being present if required. Any actions arising from the discussion are recorded; the adviser offers to do this, making clear that responsibility for *implementing* the action rests with the boss and the manager.

There is nothing especially extraordinary about the kinds of developmental actions which have resulted, although, as is to be expected, they tend to be highly specific to the individual. Examples include the use of special projects, membership of an important committee or working party, attendance at a management course, and individual work such as analysing the use of time or managerial behaviour at meetings.

counselling, as there are several excellent sources which the interested reader can pursue. For our purposes we adopt Barrie Hopson's[28] 'Parsimonious definition of "helping people explore problems so that they can decide what to do about them" '. An advantage of this definition is that it embraces the two broad purposes of counselling outlined above and it allows for the several schools of, or approaches to, counselling which have been devised over the years, for example psycho-analytic, behavioural, client-centred.

Though there are no relevant surveys of practice, anecdotal evidence and the professional literature indicate that the provision of counselling is on the increase. And the practical experience that organizations have had has highlighted the various issues to be faced in providing this kind of help.

Who should counsel is a particularly important issue. There are various options: the use of professional counsellors, either external or internal; the use of paraprofessional counsellors, such as personnel or other staff who have received special training in counselling skills; the use of others who practise counselling skills as a normal part of their jobs, such as line managers coaching their staff or conducting appraisal interviews.

Cutting across this issue is that of the role of the counsellor. Hopson[29] argues that the counsellor must have a clearly defined contract with the organization concerning job definition, confidentiality and loyalty. The counsellor's loyalties may be divided between organization and clients – indeed, if the organization is putting up the money, it may believe itself to be the client; hence the importance of working out a contract at the outset. The counsellor may experience role conflict in trying to meet the needs of both organization and individuals. Watts[30] suggests, however, that 'often this role conflict will not present any practical difficulties, either because the interests of the client and the organization are not in opposition, or because the counsellor's role is sufficiently understood within the organization to allow him to address the client's interests without fear of recrimination'.

But this is to look at the role of the counsellor primarily from the counsellor's viewpoint. To thoroughly understand this role it is necessary to consider the perspective of the organization (as employer) and the perceptions of the employees. As hinted at above, an organization may see counselling as another management tool serving organizational ends. This being so, any role conflict might be expected to be resolved in favour of the organization. Our own experience[31] of an organizational career counselling scheme which uses trained personnel staff as counsellors provides one example where this is true and the personnel officers see their role primarily in organizational terms. Perhaps this means that the personnel officers are not, in fact, operating as counsellors even though they are using counselling skills.

Considering now the individual's point of view, the client's perception of the role of the counsellor will be influenced by a number of factors, including the information provided by the organization about counselling, the behaviour of the counsellor, and the individual's own particular attitudes. As Watts[32] suggests, clients may feel reticent about opening up too much if they feel that the counsellor is there to manipulate them on the organization's behalf, or if they feel that the information they disclose may be used against them in some way. Geoffrey Sworder,[33] from ICI, considers that this problem is likely to be particularly acute if the counsellor is in personnel and clearly a part of management. Our research[34] lends some support for Sworder's view: in our evaluation of the career conselling scheme to which we referred a moment ago we found that individuals saw the counsellors – personnel officers – as part of management.

These issues, and others associated with them – for example, provision of training, costs – cannot be resolved straightforwardly. The resolution of them can itself be looked on as an issue – that of evaluation. Even if the purposes and objectives of the counselling provision are clearly stated, as they must be, evaluation is difficult enough; where such statements are absent, the task naturally is more difficult still. Subjective evaluation, based on the reactions of the various parties involved, is likely to remain the primary basis for assessing the worth of counselling provision. Provided this is carried out in a systematic fashion, we can learn much from it, as Example 4.9 shows.

Assessment centres   The examples given in this chapter of how ACs are used indicate their potential value for developmental purposes. This potential is being exploited more and more in the UK and we have followed the US trend towards 'development centres' – in other words ACs used *primarily* for training and development purposes. Even where ACs are used mainly as a device for assessing potential it has to be recognized , that participation in itself may be of developmental value. For example, assessees can get a better under-standing of what a manager does and of the qualities needed to be a successful manager. They learn about their strengths and weaknesses and become better equipped to make more informed decisions about their development. Obviously this developmental value is increased if feedback on performance is provided to the participant. As with appraisal schemes, the disclosure of information is a sensitive issue for organizations using ACs chiefly for administrative purposes.

It is worth noting that there may be developmental value in ACs not only for the assessees, but also for the assessors. A properly established AC will include an assessors' training programme to make the managers better skilled at observing and assessing performance. They may carry these skills with them to the management of their day-to-day tasks. Their interviewing skills may also be improved. There is an opportunity cost involved in the participation of assessors and assessees, but there are potential side-benefits here too because their absence from the office may create a development opportunity for someone else. For instance, a manager participating in some way in an AC may be able to delegate duties to a subordinate (or subordinates) during the period of absence.

Providing career information
As an end to this chapter a few sentences are in order on the provision of career information – one of the deficiencies in much of career

Example 4.9   *Career development counselling – an experiment and an evaluation*

The experimental career counselling programme described here arose out of discussions between representatives of various sections of the Manpower Services Commission and of Sundridge Park Management Centre and the Centre for Professional and Executive Career Development (CEPEC). The discussions centred on whether counselling could steer unemployed people into suitable Government sponsored training for the benefit of their future careers and, more broadly, whether counselling would help people to find suitable jobs and find them more quickly. Consequently, a programme was devised with the following aims:

a   To help unemployed Professional and Executive Register (PER) registrants in their search for suitable employment (for example: improved understanding of personal strengths and weaknesses; improved self-presentation at interview; improved job-finding tactics, information about the jobs market and available training).

b   To enable these people to come to a realistic understanding of their employment opportunities and so to aim for a job which is compatible with these.

c   To reduce the time it takes these people to find a suitable job.

d   To estimate the likely demand for a career counselling service for PER registrants.

The counselling process as practised at CEPEC has five main stages:

1   Pre-counselling – information is supplied by PER to CEPEC.

2   Survey of the client's situation – this is the first face-to-face meeting between the counsellor and client. It begins with the counsellor describing the counselling process and establishing a formal understanding with the client. The survey of the client's situation will range over both career related and domestic matters and usually results in the identification of areas where counselling is needed.

3   Counselling (understood by CEPEC as 'helping people to help themselves') either about personal or career matters, or both.

4   Guidance, such as information giving (jobs, careers, training) or referral (further professional help).

5   Follow-up, by postal questionnaire after three months and by reference to PER records after twelve months.

Typically, these stages would extend over at least two counselling sessions, the first session after being taken up entirely by the survey of the client's situation. A personality inventory may also be used at the end of the first session and discussed at the next meeting with the client. The ninety-nine people who participated in the experimental programme received between them a total of 273 counselling sessions, the average length of a session being an hour and three quarters. Clients received between one and a half and eighteen and a half hours of counselling, the average being five hours. As well as the counselling sessions, clients were expected to do some work in their own time, for example, self-analysis, preparing or improving a *curriculum vitae* according to guidelines given on an information sheet. Closed circuit TV was available for clients to see themselves performing in simulated job interviews. This facility was taken up by forty-seven clients. The counselling was provided by trained and experienced CEPEC counsellors.

The ninety-nine clients in the experimental group (the number had been larger originally, but some dropped out for various reasons) were matched with a control group of PER registrants who did not receive counselling. Comparisons between the two groups were made three months after each pair of individuals (one from the experimental group matched with a comparable individual from the control group) joined the experiment and a further follow-up took place twelve months after joining.

Results from the three-month follow up provided evidence that:

- the counselled group was more active in looking for jobs (more jobs applications, more interviews received) than those who had not been counselled

- most of those who had received counselling felt that it had been useful (improved self-marketing, increased morale and confidence, clearer career direction)

- a majority of those who had found a job or had gone on to further training felt that the counselling had helped with this.

Results from the twelve-month follow-up showed that those who had received counselling found employment more quickly than those from the control group, although there was no difference between the two groups as regards the number of jobs obtained.

management activity. It is true that many of the activities described in this chapter have an information-giving function, and internal advertising of job vacancies is a common method. But there are other possibilities too, such as booklets about career opportunities. Included under this heading would be catalogues of training activities, for example. But how widely are such catalogues, and similar guides, distributed within the organization? A more ambitious approach, however, would be for an organization to provide information booklets about its fields of work – what it is like to work in a particular function, what sort of training is required, what the career paths are. Films or videotapes can also be used for this purpose. Still more innovative would be the use of computer technology; this is one of the challenges and opportunities to which we shall turn in Chapter 8.

Summary

In this chapter, the relative strengths and weaknesses of less common approaches to appraisal and career development have been examined. First, methods of assessing past performance were reviewed: personality ratings, narratives or essays, critical incidents, and new rating methods like behaviourally anchored rating scales and behavioural observation scales. The use of appraisal systems, psychological tests and assessment centres were next looked at as means of assessing potential. Assessment centres were also considered from a development point of view; they are one way in which individuals might be involved in their appraisal and development, the third main topic covered here. Reviewed under this heading are subordinate participation in appraisal, self-development and self-directed learning, methods of employee involvement and their benefits, counselling and the provision of career information.

References

1 D. Gill, *Appraising Performance: Present Trends and the Next Decade*, IPM Information Report No. 25 (Institute of Personnel Management 1977).

2 P.B. Warr and M.W. Bird, *Identifying Supervisory Training Needs* (HMSO 1968).

3 S. Fineman and R. Payne, 'Applications of behavioural rating scales: some reliability and validity findings', *Industrial Relations Journal*, **5** (1974), pp. 38–44.

4 J.G. Goodale and R.J. Burke, 'Behaviourally based rating scales need not be job specific' *Journal of Applied Psychology*, **60** (1975) pp. 389–91.

5 G.P. Latham and K.N. Wexley, *Increasing Productivity Through Performance Appraisal* (Addison-Wesley 1981).

6 A. Stewart and V. Stewart, *Tomorrow's Managers Today* (2nd edn) (Institute of Personnel Management 1981).

7 Latham and Wexley, *Increasing Productivity Through Performance Appraisal*.

8 P. Long, *Performance Approval Revisited* (Institute of Personnel Management 1986).
Gill, *Appraising Performance: Present Trends and the Next Decade*.
R.F. Holdsworth, *Identifying Managerial Potential*, Management Survey Report No. 27 (British Institute of Management 1975).

9 Validation is dealt with in a companion volume in this series: C. Lewis, *Employee Selection* (Stanley Thornes 1991).

10 V. Dulewicz, 'Improving assessment centres', *Personnel Management*, June (1991), pp. 50–55.

11 J. Burgoyne, T. Boydell and M. Pedler, *Self Development Theory and Applications for Practitioners* (The Association of Teachers of Management).

12 M. Pedler and T. Boydell, 'What is self-development?', in T. Boydell and M. Pedler, *Management Self-Development* (Gower 1981).

13 M. Berger and B. Nixon, 'Management development at Sun Alliance', in B. Nixon (ed.), *New Approaches to Management Development* (Gower, for the Association of Teachers of Management, 1981).

14   J. Fairbairns, Evaluation of *Wider Opportunities for Women ('WOW') Courses: Final Report* (Manpower Services Commission 1979).

15   Burgoyne, Boydell and Pedler, *Self Development: Theory and Applications for Practitioners.*

16   Local Government Training Board, *Could You Be a Better Manager?* (Local Government Training Board 1977).

17   M. Pedler, J. Burgoyne and T. Boydell, *A Manager's Guide to Self-Development*, 2nd ed. (McGraw-Hill 1986).

18   M. Woodcock and D. Francis, *The Unblocked Manager: A Practical Guide to Self-Development* (Gower 1982).

19   J. Burgoyne and C. Germaine, 'Career Self-Management and Personal Development' *Personnel Management* (April 1984).

20   Some North American workbooks are:
D. Campbell, *If You Don't Know Where You're Going, You'll Probably End Up Somewhere Else* (Argus Communications, Nile, Ill. 1974).
E.L. Adams, Jr., *Career Advancement Guide* (McGraw-Hill 1975).
W.D. Storey, *Career Dimensions*, Vols. I and II (General Electric Company, Croton-on-Hudson, New York, 1976).

21   R.G. Harrison, 'Life goals planning and interpersonal skill development: A programme for middle managers in the British Civil Service' *Personnel Review*, **8** (1979), pp. 40–43.

22   W.D. Storey, (ed.), *A Guide for Career Development Inquiry*, ASTD Research Series Paper No.2 (American Society for Training and Development, Madison, Wisc.,1979)

23   J.A. Miller, cited in R.S. Williams, *Career Management and Career Planning* (HMSO 1982).

24   ibid.

25   Fairbairns, *Evaluation of 'WOW' Courses*.
Harrison, 'Life goals planning and interpersonal skill development'.
R.S. Williams, 'Developing skills for women in middle management: Final report on course evaluation' (Management and Personnel Office, London, 1983).
M. Povall, 'Report on First "Managerial Effectiveness for Women" Course 1982' (The City University Business School, London, 1982)

26   R. S. Williams, *Career Management and Career Planning* (HMSO 1981).

27   A. Mumford, 'Counselling senior managers' development', in T. Boydell and M. Pedler (eds.), *Management Self-Development* (Gower 1981).

28   B. Hopson, 'Counselling in work settings', in P.B. Warr (ed.), *Psychology at Work* (2nd edn) (Penguin 1978).

29   B. Hopson 'Techniques and methods of counselling', in A.G. Watts (ed.), *Counselling at Work* (Bedford Square Press 1977).

30   A.G. Watts, 'Counselling resources outside the organisation', in A.G. Watts (ed.), *Counselling at Work*.

31   C.A. Fletcher and R.S. Williams, 'Interviewee perceptions of an organisational careers guidance scheme', *British Journal of Guidance and Counselling*, **8** (1980), pp. 57–66.

32   Watts, *Counselling at Work*.

33   G. Sworder, 'Problems for the counsellor in his task' in A.G. Watts (ed.), *Counselling at Work*.

34   C.A. Fletcher and R.S. Williams, 'Interviewee perceptions of an organisational careers guidance scheme'.

5
Devising and implementing appraisal systems

No stage in an appraisal system's life is more vital than its inception. Many failures are traced back to such things as defining inappropriate objectives for the scheme, inadequate preliminary consultation with users, and so on. As in other things, if you do not get your product right (or very nearly right) in the first place, and launch it correctly, the returns will be predictably low. So, in this chapter we shall concentrate on ways of devising and implementing performance appraisal. In contrast to the previous chapters which have been more concerned with what has happened previously and what tends to happen now, this one will be much more direct in saying what general approach should be adopted. Despite this more direct advice, however, we hope not to fall into the trap of trying to tell you what is or is not the best form of appraisal system – for that depends on many factors specific to each organization. But much of what needs to be said about the operation of appraisal systems applies to many different types of system.

Devising the system: objectives, criteria, forms

The process usually starts with the personnel department or some other central body perceiving the need for a new or revamped appraisal scheme. Sometimes this diagnosis is based on evidence – appraisals not being done, or being done very late, appraisal forms being less than informative in their content, complaints from line managers, and so on. Just as often it is based on vague notions that 'it is time for a change' or 'the whole thing needs shaking up'. Where there has been no formal appraisal system previously, the situation is reasonably straightforward (but this does not mean easy). Where there has been an appraisal programme which has been perceived as failing, things are more tricky; there is a temptation to change everything about the appraisal scheme, which may be neither desirable nor necessary. In this case a careful examination of all the aspects of the existing system is worthwhile; there may be a baby somewhere in there with the bathwater! However, given the situation of a completely fresh start, where does one begin?

The first thing to be settled is the purpose of the system – what are the objectives to be? Assessment and feedback? Motivation and performance improvement? Comparability and an equitable reward system? Is it to be biased towards the needs of the organization or will it also try to meet the needs of the individual? If it ignores the latter totally it is unlikely that the prognosis will be good, so some effort to find out what individual needs are is worthwhile. This means consultation at an early stage with the trade unions, or staff associations and, ideally, some more systematic attempt at gathering information on employees' needs, for example by a questionnaire survey. It may well be that different groups (for example, professional versus managerial) or levels of employees have quite different needs in this respect. Consultation with the managers who will be doing the appraisals (or their representatives) is at least equally important. The success of the scheme depends heavily on them, and their ideas on the objectives and techniques should be noted – some feeling of ownership of the scheme is likely to increase their commitment to it, a vital factor that cannot be over-emphasized. In organization X (Case study 1, page 33) more than half of the senior managers were consulted about the new appraisal scheme through a series of discussion groups, and this is perhaps as good a way as any to get such an input. Consultation along these lines can play a part in clarifying the strengths and weaknesses of existing appraisal practices too. There may be occasions, of course, when the views elicited through consultation run counter to the initial ideas and plans of the personnel specialists; to consult the participants of appraisal and subsequently ignore their views will probably prove more disastrous than not having consulted them at all – so there has to be some flexibility and openness of mind and a willingness to negotiate aims if the consultation process is to be worthwhile.

In the process of defining the objectives of the scheme, one is also by implication deciding to some extent on the methods and criteria that will be used. So, for example, if it is decided that performance improvement is the key objective, the choice of method is more likely to be the results-orientated rather than the ratings approach, the latter being more associated with the objective of evaluating and comparing employees. And it follows that this choice would determine the type of criteria – in this case task achievements of some kind – and who will set them (the manager doing the appraisal, in conjunction with the subordinate). But the objectives defined for the scheme only imply the choice of performance criteria in general terms. Some method of deriving the specific criteria to be used is required. Basically this means job analysis. Jobs can be analysed in terms of a whole host of dimensions, of which there are three main types relevant to performance appraisal and to other personnel purposes:

● Job- or task-orientated, which emphasizes work outcomes or activities.

- Worker-orientated, which emphasizes the behaviour of the job-holder.

- Abilities-orientated, which focuses on the underlying abilities or aptitudes required to perform the job.

There is some degree of overlap between these three types and in any event it is unlikely that any one type is entirely satisfactory as a basis for your job analysis exercise. Exactly how many dimensions are chosen will depend in large part upon the purposes to which the job analysis information will be put. You might choose to kill several birds with one stone and generate information relevant not only to performance appraisal but also to promotion procedures and to the identification of training needs. This being so, it may be appropriate to employ a wide range of dimensions in the job analysis. The risk, though, is that the resulting information may be of some relevance to a wide range of purposes but is not optimally relevant to any one particular purpose. Inevitably, the decision will be a trade-off: one rather general purpose job analysis or several tailor-made analyses.

Having decided the purpose of the analysis and the types of job dimensions to be studied – the nature and level of the job are obvious considerations here – the next step is to decide how to get the information. The methods available include direct observation, diaries, interviews, and questionnaires, and each has its strengths and weaknesses. *Direct observation*, for example, is highly time-consuming on the part of the observer or analyst and for some jobs – managerial ones in particular – it may not be possible to observe the job-holder all of the time, for instance the manager may work during journeys to and from home or while at home. On the other hand, direct observation can be a very rich source of data about the way in which jobs are carried out and can thereby serve to correct some of the deficiencies of the other methods. For example, studies of managerial work have reported discrepancies between what managers say they do and what they actually do.

Another direct method of obtaining information from the job-holder is to use some kind of *self-completion diary*: Rosemary Stewart's[1] studies of managerial work represent a particularly good example. Depending upon the design of the diary, this approach can generate comprehensive information about job activities, who was involved, the duration of the activity, its outcome and frequency. The diary might be kept every day for a week or two or two days a week for a longer period. A particular difficulty, here, though, is that diaries are time-consuming to complete, and as such they may be unacceptable to the job-holder – particularly to busy managers.

A variant of this approach is the *critical incident diary* which we described in Chapter 4 as an appraisal method. It also has applications for job analysis purposes, such as establishing criteria to distinguish between effective and ineffective performance – clearly of relevance to performance appraisal and promotion procedures. One way of using this approach might be as follows. At the end of each day the job-holder would complete the diary by describing two incidents: the one which had caused the most difficulty during the day and the one which had been most successful (from the job-holder's point of view). To aid completion of the diary it may be helpful to give some guidelines – who else was involved, how frequently does this type of incident occur, etc. Again the diary might be kept each day for a week or two or on random days over a longer period. Like the self-completion diary this too is rather time-consuming for the job-holder to complete. It is also time-consuming for the analyst to actually analyse the information yielded. The approach is heavily dependent upon the writing skills of the job-holder but well-written incidents certainly provide very graphic accounts of aspects of the job(s) being studied.

Interviews range from fully structured to completely unstructured, though at least some degree of structure is likely to be needed. The content of the interview schedule would depend upon a number of factors – the purpose(s) to which the information will be put, the nature of the job being studied, and what other (if any) methods were being used. This too is quite a time-consuming approach, though less so than those described so far, both in terms of carrying out the interviews and of analysing the information obtained. This is particularly true if the number of interviews to be carried out is large. A variation on this theme is the group interview or group discussion in which the analyst leads a discussion amongst, say, five to seven holders of the same job. Using these approaches, however, a skilled interviewer can build up a good picture of how the job-holders go about their work – or, at least, how they say they go about their work – what their problems are, what they enjoy in their work, what skills and knowledge they require or believe they require for effective performance, and so on.

Under the heading of interview we might also consider the *repertory grid* approach. This was originally developed in the field of clinical psychology but it has proved to be an immensely flexible and adaptable technique that has many applications in the personnel field.[2] Basically, it is a way of getting a picture of the way an individual sees events, people or things in his world. The way one might use it in deriving performance criteria is something like this: you would ask a senior manager to list several subordinates who were effective in their jobs and several who were ineffective. Then you would present the manager with the names of three of them (say, two effective and one not) and ask him to specify in what way two of them were alike – apart from overall effectiveness – and different from the third. The manager might say that two have a good grasp of figures whereas the third did not. You would then ask the manager to apply this 'construct' (good with figures or not) to all the other subordinates in the list. After that, another three names would be drawn and the procedure repeated – in what way are two of them alike and different from the third? By continuing this process you would eventually end up with a list of constructs or dimensions that the manager used for differentiating between effective and ineffective performers. Some simple types of analyses of this information would soon reveal the extent to which the manager was using many different words for the same few ways of describing the differences between the sheep and the goats. Carry out the same process for a group of senior managers, pool the results, and you get the dimensions that might most usefully be incorporated into the appraisal rating scales. This, of course, is only a very brief sketch of the repertory grid technique; for a very clear introduction to it, the reader is referred to Shaw and McKnight.[3] The beauty of this method is that it allows individual managers to articulate their views in such a way as to let them use their *own* descriptive terms, rather than trying to force them to use a set of dimensions dreamed up by somebody else and which may be much less meaningful to them.

Questionnaires can take various forms. One approach would be to have a series of 'open' questions (rather like a structured interview schedule) for completion by the manager. Like the interview, this method generates a tremendous amount of information which is time-consuming to analyse. At the opposite extreme would be questionnaires made up of, say, lists of activities or behavioural statements describing the job. This highly structured approach entails a lot of development work – probably using one or more of the methods described so far – but such questionnaires often do not take much time to complete and they are likely to be suitable for computer analysis.

Given that the method used to some extent determines the kind of information generated – and hence the adequacy of the job analysis – it is unlikely that one method alone will be sufficient. The precise combination of methods will, as implied earlier, depend upon the purpose of the analysis and the type of job! It is also probable that one source of information – the job-holder – will be insufficient. The other sources that can be tapped include the job-holder's immediate superior and higher levels of management, peers, and possibly subordinates. By drawing upon multiple sources of information and using a number of methods it is possible to achieve a more comprehensive understanding of the way in which job-holders actually carry out their work, how they believe they carry out their work, and how they should carry out their work.

From the mass of information generated, the next step is to derive performance criteria for the appraisal system. Exactly how you go about this will depend upon the type of information generated. Qualitative material obtained from interviews, for example, lends itself to content analysis. Analysis of quantitative data may vary in sophistication from simple frequency counts through to highly complex statistical techniques such as factor analysis or cluster analysis. Though very involved, these more complex techniques have their advantages because they help to answer the question of how many appraisal forms will be needed. Will one form suit all jobs in the organization? Or are there job families, each one sufficiently different from the others to require a separate form? The number of forms to be used and the content of those forms are fundamental questions; answers to them can be sought through job analysis. For more detailed advice on methods the reader is referred to Stewart and Stewart.[4]

Once the objectives and the performance criteria are settled, it is possible to have a shot at a preliminary draft of the appraisal form. As was noted in discussing the 'Identikit' appraisal system, most organizations have wisely opted for a form of not more than four pages. The nature and balance of the content will obviously be dictated by the chief objectives of the appraisal system, but a couple of general points are worth making here. If rating scales are used, do not make them too long – there is a limit to the number of meaningful discriminations an individual can make anyway; between five and seven points is the maximum. And providing a middle category can be asking for trouble, unless you are desperate to achieve a normal distribution of ratings (by no means guaranteed even with a middle category). A forced-choice scale – that is, one which has no middle category, thus forcing the rater to at least make a choice between the broadly favourable and the broadly unfavourable – with six categories seems to be the best option in many instances. On the other hand, if an objective-setting approach is employed, the appraiser should be discouraged both on the form and in his training from setting too many objectives. Finally, as far as designing the form is concerned, the actual layout and presentation of such documents is a neglected art form. All too often they manage to combine a distinct lack of visual appeal with an inefficient or inappropriate use of space. Perhaps there is a case for bringing in a good graphic designer and letting him or her design the layout, after having been given the essential requirements. Whatever the problems of appraisal, there is no need for the forms to be so badly designed and to look so cheerless!

Devising the system: the wider context

So far, design of appraisal systems has been looked at in terms of defining objectives and of some of the issues arising out of that process. Attention now needs to be given to other factors that need reviewing when deciding on the length, content and flexibility of the report form, the timing of the appraisals, who does them, and the degree of central or local control of the system.

The organizational style

It has been argued,[5] with some justification, that different styles of appraisal are needed for organizations of varying types. Thus, the heavily bureaucratic, stable organization might reasonably adopt a relatively formal appraisal scheme incorporating detailed appraisal forms, regular yearly appraisal and a considerable degree of central control. On the other hand, an organization operating in a fast-changing area like high technology might itself undergo rapid changes in the development of staff and in its internal structure. Here, appraisal would need to be more flexible, both in content and timing, and be more subject to local (line management) control. The emphasis might be more on development than on assessment.

The management structure

This helps to determine who does the appraisal and when. A 'flattened pyramid' structure will mean that towards the lower end of the scale each manager will have a large number of subordinates, so the task of appraisal almost inevitably falls on the first-line supervisor ('father'). Even then, the numbers involved may be such that appraisals have to be staggered over the whole year, or even given less often than annually. When there are variations in management structure, different levels of appraiser or a different periodicity may be needed to keep the whole thing manageable. However, the question might also be asked whether an individual who has so many subordinates as to be unable to appraise them over a six-week period can in fact be in any position to manage them properly on a day-to-day basis anyway.

Geographical spread

The amount of contact managers have with subordinates based elsewhere inevitably affects appraisal. Sometimes separation makes appraisal all the more necessary, but it usually makes it more difficult because of the lack of contact between the parties. This is one of the ironies of appraisal – when it is most needed (where communication is poor), it is also most difficult to do. Unfortunately, there is a tendency to see appraisal as a panacea for poor communication; thus, an oft-repeated claim one hears on appraisal training courses is that if we had managers who communicated with staff frequently, appraisal would be unnecessary. This is just not the case: research shows that it is precisely those managers who have higher levels of communication with their staff who have the most productive appraisal interviews, while their less communicative counterparts achieve much less with their interviews[6] (see Figure 3). Taking all this into account, it would seem sensible, where managers and appraisees are located on different sites far apart, to check whether any superior on the spot sees the individual's performance more regularly and so might be at least partly involved in the appraisal. Failing this, the frequency of appraisal might be increased, or Latham and Wexley's[7] suggestion that self-appraisal be used in such circumstances might be taken up.

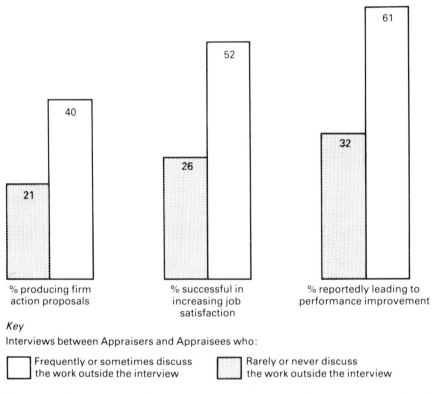

Key
Interviews between Appraisers and Appraisees who:

☐ Frequently or sometimes discuss the work outside the interview   ▨ Rarely or never discuss the work outside the interview

Figure 3   *Frequency of appraiser-appraisee job discussion outside the interview related to three indicators of how effective the appraisal interview has been*

The level of the appraisees

As we have seen, some organizations involve only certain management groups in appraisal. Experience suggests that appraisal can work well with all sorts of groups – telephonists, nurses, secretaries, policemen – and not just managers. However, the appraisal may meet different needs both for the organization and for the individual at different levels. For example, routine low-level clerical jobs scarcely require a complex appraisal form. This does not mean, however, that they are not worth appraising. But the content, style and frequency may be different. Thus, some jobs, such as those of typists and machine operators, by their nature provide feedback on performance, and deficiencies can usually be detected and attempts made to remedy them as soon as they occur; so an appraisal based chiefly on performance review could be of dubious value. The purposes of appraisal at junior levels are likely to be more in the nature of giving recognition for the work done, letting appraisees give their own views or ideas about the work and (where appropriate) talking about the possibilities of career progression. Age, too, is a relevant factor here; younger staff with potential may need more frequent appraisal, while staff nearer retirement may have much less wish and need to be appraised. And less experienced staff, new to the organization, also tend to need appraisal more frequently – regardless of age.

Linking in with other personnel management systems
How appraisal will mesh in with the promotion, training and career development systems, and in some cases the financial reward system too (though the less the connection with this the better), must be considered at the design stage. As we have shown already, the linkages can be very extensive and, quite apart from the general purposes we have just mentioned, there are still others. For example, the appraisal system may have a part to play in disciplinary and dismissal procedures, and in this context it is worth noting that disclosure of appraisal reports can be requested in, say, sex or race discrimination cases.

Appraisal schemes typically are multi-purpose, but whether such a scheme is optionally successful for any one purpose remains open to question. It is often said that line managers knowing they are going to have to conduct an appraisal interview will inflate ratings and write less than informative narratives. If the accuracy of appraisals can be questioned in this way then their value for administrative purposes, such as pay or promotion systems, must likewise be questionable. But the very use of appraisal data for administrative purposes may itself act as an inflationary pressure, hence the link between appraisal and administrative purposes may be self-defeating. Such considerations as these have led some organizations to reduce their reliance on appraisals and adopt other methods, for example the use of assessment centres to assess potential. Some organizations have split their appraisal system, as we have seen, by having 'open' arrangements for the assessment of current performance and a 'closed' form for appraising potential. And Randell and others have suggested a further split – having a separate appraisal system for the determination of pay rewards. Such arrangements raise other considerations of course: the need for separate documentation, possibly an extra work load for the line managers, the possibility of inconsistent appraisals, the need for extra training, and so on. Inevitably, then, the decision once again will be something of a trade-off. But in considering how the appraisal system is to be linked with other systems, it is helpful to think in specific terms rather than at a level of generality such as 'we will use the appraisal in training and development'. How, exactly, will the appraisal be used for training and development purposes? As a basis for direct action by the line manager through coaching, counselling, and goal-setting? Through the statement of training needs by the line manager? And how are such statements to be used? Through the scrutiny of the appraisal form by personnel or training staff?

Thinking about design issues in such specific terms helps to avoid taking decisions in a vacuum. Another way of helping to avoid this is to gather information about how the existing system works in practice; this evidence can be used to help improve the existing system or develop a new one. And this goes for all the other systems too, not just the appraisal system. It is also worth making the point, obvious though it is, that should you be reviewing, say, the promotion system, then this may have implications for what you do in the appraisal system.

Implementing the system

Having devised the scheme, you are ready to introduce it. Again, consultation with the interested parties is no bad thing. But at this stage the motive behind consultation will be more to gain understanding and commitment than to get fresh ideas. The scheme has to be publicized in some manner for both appraisers and appraisees. Apart from written materials explaining the purpose and the procedure, which are often distributed and probably often lost or forgotten by the recipients, it is not easy to see other methods of achieving this. At senior management levels, oral presentation can be used (indeed, should be). Something similar could be done lower down, but the cost in time is rather heavy (although for new staff it can be built into the induction procedures). Whatever method is used, it is wise to stress the consultative aspects of the scheme's development and not to present it as an 'ivory-tower' personnel exercise; the participants need to see clearly what is in it for them. This will involve, amongst other things, showing them the appraisal forms and explaining the rationale behind the procedure. It is desirable to emphasize (provided it is true), that the whole thing is not inscribed on tablets of stone, and that it will be subject to evaluation processes and, if necessary, resulting modification.

Commitment and/or information-giving sessions of this kind represent the first stage of training, but the main thrust of the training effort should be kept separate. There are two components, and ideally they need to be handled as distinct training tasks, though they are best kept fairly close together in time, so far as those being trained are concerned. The first component deals with the effective and accurate observation and assessment of performance, and with putting that skill into use in completing the appraisal form. Most courses content themselves with the latter part of this – how to fill in the form correctly (which means how personnel wants it to be done). But some extra effort put in here on helping managers to minimize the typical rating errors which are made and to increase their observational and assessment skills will pay dividends far beyond appraisal itself. A detailed account of methods available is beyond the scope of the present text, but a good description can be found in Chapter 5 of Latham and Wexley.[8]

If this more general training is not feasible, case studies requiring the manager to write reports on pen-picture characters are better than just written instructions as a way of training people to complete the report properly, especially when the results are discussed with others (senior managers, peers, training officers, etc.). One organization even went as far as to provide a programmed learning booklet and associated case studies in its training of appraisers.[9] But, to reiterate, a broader workshop on observing and assessing behaviour, as well as specific exercises on completing the appraisal form – completing rating scales if these are a part of the form, or setting and assessing performance targets or objectives – are a good combination.

The other main training effort is directed towards the appraisal interview (assuming that the scheme incorporates one; some stone-age relics do not). It is essential to develop training courses that incorporate at least two practice interviews, under guidance. This means having a group of tutors available – training staff, occupational psychologists, or perhaps experienced line managers who have been trained in a small group work. The cost and difficulty entailed in this sometimes persuades organizations to send their people on standard courses; while this may be better than no training at all, it is preferable to have courses specifically tailored to the circumstances and the appraisal system of the particular organization. Where managers have not been used to carrying out appraisal interviews, this training is more essential than ever, reducing much of the anxiety they feel over conducting these interviews, and improving their handling of them. The type of appraisal system operated determines not only the type of training needed, but also the sorts of problems it will present. Appraisals which have an assessment and comparability function tend to be the ones which need greatest emphasis on interview training, because there is little doubt that conveying and/or discussing assessments with subordinates is what most appraisers find most daunting, if only prospectively. There is much guidance that can be given and tried out in practice interviews that will help with this – keeping the evaluation job-related, being sure to have evidence available to support adverse comments, encouraging self-review as the initial strategy, not mentioning more than two deficiencies in performance, balancing criticisms with recognition of work done well, and so on. Training in appraisal is a subject for a book in itself – see the references at the end of this chapter for fuller treatments of the subject.

In the same way that appraisal form training needs to be broad in scope, to include observation and assessment of performance, so, too, is there a broader aspect to appraisal interview training. Here, though, the emphasis is on enabling managers to extend appraisal interview skills to their day-to-day management, thereby seeing appraisal in the broader context of staff development. Particular appraisal skills which have day-to-day application in this way include giving feedback on performance, attentive listening, encouraging subordinate participation, etc.

Commitment meetings, training in assessment skills, sessions on how to fill in the report form, interview training – we know what some of you are thinking! But we said at the start that this chapter would be more direct in suggesting what *should* be done. What is offered here is something like a counsel of perfection, but it illustrates the point that successful appraisal cannot be had on the cheap. Organizational resources realities do of course intrude, but if your sights are set low to begin with, you can be sure that the end result will be pretty meagre too. The more you put into appraisal schemes, the more you get out of them.

Finally, if you are training people for appraisal, where do you start? The advice given is, usually, 'at the top'. And with good reason – if top management is not seen to be involved and committed, nobody else is likely to take it seriously either. Appraisal is not something that should be seen as 'good for *other* people'. Starting at the top and working down, even if done only in one section of the organization at a time, also lets top management know what it is like to be on the receiving side of appraisal, an insight which may help when they in turn carry out their appraisals.

A final aspect of implementing the scheme is the decision on who keeps appraisal information and for how long. There are organizations which expressly forbid managers to keep a copy of appraisal information – the idea being that by doing so they discourage appraisers from referring back to what they said the previous year, to justify it or to maintain a façade of consistency. Each year, the individual appraisee gets a fresh start. However, the memory powers of managers aside, the widespread availability of photocopiers has made this an increasingly forlorn policy. Moreover, if it is an objectives-orientated scheme, keeping a copy of the form is a necessity. The questions of how long appraisal reports should be kept and whether they should be passed on to others are quite another matter. Probably only the last appraisal form needs to be kept by the line manager, while Personnel will keep several years' appraisals. People and circumstances change, and hanging on to appraisal information for a long time invests it with a significance it does not warrant over such a period. This is also one of the arguments against the practice of managers passing on appraisal forms about their subordinates to their successors. This no doubt helps the new manager to settle in, and gives him or her some idea of the staff he or she has to manage. But the arrival of a new manager is in itself an important change in circumstances which might affect an individual's performance in either direction. Given the subjective element in appraisal, it is also important that managers look at their subordinates with as fresh and as unprejudiced an eye as possible. There is all too great a danger of seeing what we are led to expect to see. For these reasons, it is perhaps best to discourage the handing-on of appraisal information from outgoing to incoming managers, though it is almost impossible to stop absolutely.

Summary

You need to get appraisal schemes right from their inception. The first thing to do is to get clear what the *objectives* of the scheme are to be, which should involve discussion with all the interested parties to obtain their views and commitment. The objectives decided on will, to a large extent, dictate the methods and performance criteria for appraisal. To determine the criteria more specifically, a variety of techniques may be used in analysing the jobs – direct observation, self-completed diaries, critical incident methods, interviews, repertory grids and questionnaires. Apart from the questions of the objectives, criteria and type of form to be used, devising an appraisal system requires the designer to take account of numerous other contextual factors, such as the management structure, the organizational style, the geographical spread and grade levels of the people being appraised, and other personnel management systems. When the stage of introducing and implementing the scheme is reached, further consultation and publicity about it is desirable. Above all, *training* for appraisers, preferably including supervised practice interviews, is vital. It is also good practice to introduce the scheme at the top of the organization and work downwards.

References

1   R. Stewart, *Constrasts in Management* (McGraw-Hill 1976).
2   M. Easterby-Smith, 'How to use repertory grids in HRD,' *Journal of European Industrial Training*, **4** (1980).
    V. Stewart and A. Stewart, *Business Applications of the Repertory Grid* (McGraw-Hill 1981).
3   M.L.G. Shaw and C. McKnight, *Think Again: Personal Decision-Making and Problem-Solving* (Prentice-Hall 1981).
4   V. Stewart and A. Stewart, *Practical Performance Appraisal* (Gower 1977).
5   C. Handy, 'Organisation behaviour: organisational influences on appraisals', *Industrial and Commercial Training*, **1** (1975), pp. 326–30
6   C. A. Fletcher 'Manager/subordinate communication and leadership style: a field study of their relationship to perceived outcomes of appraisal interviews' *Personnel Review*, **1** (1978), pp. 59–62.
7   G.P. Latham and K.N. Wexley, *Increasing Productivity Through Performance Appraisal* (Addison-Wesley 1981).
8   Latham and Wexley, *Increasing Productivity Through Performance Appraisal*.
9   D. Lodge, 'The design of a learning package', *Industrial Training International*, **8** (1973), pp. 123–7.
10   G.A. Randell, P.M.A. Packard, R.L. Shaw and A.T. Slater, *Staff Appraisal* (Institute of Personnel Management 1974).
    C. Lewis, N. Edgerton and R. Parkinson, 'Interview training: finding the facts and minding the feelings', *Personnel Management* (May 1976), pp. 29–33.
    E. Anstey, C. Fletcher and J. Walker, *Staff Appraisal and Development* (George Allen and Unwin 1976).
    C.W. Allinson, 'Training in performance appraisal interviewing: an evaluation study', *Journal of Management Studies*, **14** (1977), pp. 179–91.
    N.Rackham and T.Morgan, *Behaviour Analysis and Training* (McGraw-Hill 1976).

6
Maintenance and evaluation

Once it is off the ground and going, even the best system needs a lot of care and attention, particularly in the early stages. If one looks on personnel management as a *management function*, like say, finance, then a control mechanism is needed. In this chapter we consider control mechanisms for appraisal and for other career development systems.

Two 'care and maintenance' activities appropriate to appraisal are monitoring reporting standards and keeping a check on action recommendations coming out of the appraisals. The reporting standards might be looked at in terms of the distribution of ratings (if used) – are they excessively skewed or bunched together at the centre, or do they differ wildly from one section of the organization to another? The quality of the written comments can similarly be gauged in terms of their relevance to the aims of the appraisal and the degree of information they actually impart. Thus, it is necessary to monitor standards in relation to the purposes to which the information will be put. So, if, for example, 15 per cent or 3 per cent of staff are rated as exceptional performers, what are the implications of these proportions for the promotion system? If 40 per cent of staff are seen as having no potential for further advancement, what are the implications of this for staff deployment? Should the organization be encouraging mobility of staff so as to enhance flexibility and motivation?

This elementary monitoring of written appraisals can be done by Personnel and to some extent by senior managers, who should be encouraged to take a keen interest in their subordinates' reporting standards. In the long run, however, perhaps the best way of ensuring that appraisal is done well and conscientiously is to make it one of the tasks that the managers themselves are formally assessed on. DeVries and McCall[1] note that appraisal is often treated as a minor, unrewarded task. The amount of time and effort spent on it, the effect it has on the appraisees and their careers, and its potential contribution to the organization all indicate that appraisal should be regarded as one of the most vital and direct contributions a manager can make, and should be assessed as such.

Another vital element in the maintenance of appraisal is the following up of action recommendations arising out of the interview.

There is probably no quicker way for an appraisal scheme to be discredited than for it to generate recommendations on training, transfer and so on, which are not acted on as soon as is appropriate. Regular checks are needed to see that recommendations have been carried out, and, if they have proved to be impossible to achieve, that the individual concerned has been told why. One organization's answer to this was to introduce a simple 'action sheet' which had headings for action to be taken by the appraisee, appraiser, senior management, and Personnel, with a space after each for the agreed action to be written in. Copies of the sheet were given to all relevant parties. It was stressed that action recommendations were not a requirement as such – some appraisals quite justifiably might well produce none. However, even when there was nothing of this kind to report, the nil return still had to be made to the personnel division, the form being signed by both appraiser and appraisee. Apart from being a record of agreed action, this simple sheet of paper was a way of checking that the appraisal interview had actually taken place. It is not unknown for managers to let the conducting of appraisal interviews slip out of their minds, and this procedure was an effective antidote to that. Personnel set up a monitoring process which put into effect recommendations that came within their sphere (for example, attendance on an external training course) and reviewed at regular intervals any suggestion for action which was to take place at a later date.

A study of the use of such a system showed that over 80 per cent of the action sheets contained some recommendations (on average, about two for each individual), most of which were – quite appropriately – for the appraiser and appraisee to deal with rather than any one else. Where something was requested of, or suggested to, Personnel (as it was in nearly 40 per cent of cases), it was expressed in clear and specific terms.

The use of a separate sheet rather like that just described can be found in appraisal schemes which emphasize the staff development objectives rather than administrative purposes. They can vary in sophistication from the simple (as described above) to ones which encourage some kind of goal-setting or action planning. But whatever the format, the important point is that it is used and that a control mechanism exists for checking that it is used. The responsibility for this rests just as much with the individual being appraised as with Personnel or line management. This is also true for making sure that agreed action actually takes place.

Not all organizations choose to use some kind of separate form for recording action; sometimes the appraisal form itself is meant to suffice. But the need for a control system is no less important. This goes too for checking that the appraisal interview takes place – getting the individual to sign the form to confirm that the interview has happened is an approach which is sometimes adopted.

Keeping an eye on reporting standards, action recommendations, and so on, is both part of maintaining a scheme and of a process of evaluating it; we shall have more to say about comprehensive evaluation shortly. If deficiencies are noted, then of course remedial action can be taken. So, for example, where appraisal forms are not being completed properly, some form of training or counselling of appraisers may be desirable. Sometimes this action will amount to little more than tinkering with the system. Later, it may involve a more fundamental review.

A different aspect of maintaining appraisal systems is the problem of commitment. A lot of effort goes into getting the whole thing going in the first place, but the impetus has to be kept up – otherwise there is a danger of the appraisal scheme becoming ritualized and taken for granted. One method that has been found useful in this context is Group Feedback Analysis.[1] A simple version of this might involve ten to twelve appraisers being asked to meet with a representative from Personnel to review the progress of the appraisal system after eighteen months or two years. A brief questionnaire on certain key aspects of the system would be completed by the line managers first, and the group's combined results fed back to them as a stimulus to, and framework for, discussion. Doing this with groups of managers helps keep interest active and reinforces the appraisers' feelings of ownership of the scheme.

The Machiavellian way of organizing such groups is to try to ensure beforehand that at least a majority of the membership of each group is favourable to appraisal, so isolating and hopefully influencing the 'awkward squad' who are less than enthusiastic about their appraisal commitments. You certainly do not want to get large numbers of 'antis' together if you can avoid it, as they will only reinforce each other's prejudices.

Group feedback exercises of this kind are a two-way communication exercise, for they throw up a lot of useful information about how the appraisal system is working. Thus, it can be looked on as part of the evaluation process, to which we now turn our attention.

Evaluating appraisal schemes

There is an unfortunate tendency for organizations which have put a lot into the setting up of their appraisal scheme to then close their eyes to the possibility that it might not all go perfectly thereafter. Indeed, one of the problems of putting a lot into an appraisal system at the outset is that a degree of inertia is built in, nobody being keen to recognize or rectify any faulty aspects of a system that took so much time and effort in the first place. And of course those organizations that did not bother much about the way appraisal was implemented are even less likely to notice when it goes wrong. Yet monitoring the progress of such systems is vital to their effectiveness, and not to do so after investing resources in developing them is particularly irrational.

What are the purposes of evaluation? Well, some of them – and some of the methods of evaluation – were dealt with when we described the monitoring of appraisal standards and the following-up of action recommendations. That kind of evaluation cannot be kept separate from the day-to-day maintenance of the system. Of concern to us here is the assessment of the extent to which the appraisals are being carried out in a manner satisfactory to appraisers and appraisees and are perceived by these parties to be producing positive results. In effect, this largely becomes an evaluation of the appraisal interview as the key interface in the appraisal process. Was it handled in the way advocated in the appraiser's training? Did it cover all the necessary topics? What level of participation did the interviewee have? What were the perceived short- and long-term effects? Answers to questions of these kinds are needed fairly soon after the start of any scheme, because if any weakness exists it can quickly lead the whole scheme to fall into disrepute before any remedial action is taken.

More broadly, we shall be concerned with the evaluation of the appraisal scheme in relation to the other career development systems which it feeds. And this in turn will lead us on to consider one particular purpose of evaluation, namely the monitoring of the personnel policies in the context of equal employment opportunity.

Evaluation techniques

Leaving aside academic studies of appraisal and the methods they have used, which in some cases are inappropriate to the normal aims of evaluation, the main techniques are:

- Interviewing appraisers and appraisees (singly or in groups)
- Analysing written reports of interviews
- Questionnaires to participants in the appraisal

The first of these has the advantages that it is flexible and can provide rich information. It has the marked disadvantage that it does not afford the respondents anonymity and this may influence the degree of frankness of the response. And if it is used, some kind of structure and quantification of the material coming out is desirable, so perhaps it is best combined with the questionnaire method.

The second approach, where it is feasible, demands some expertise in content analysis[3] techniques and can be fairly time-consuming; by its nature, it can give only a limited amount of information and will tell you little, if anything, about the way the appraisal interview was carried out. So, by and large, the questionnaire method has the most to offer in this situation – it enables the personnel department to collect the responses of a large sample of appraisers and appraisees about various aspects of the system in such a way that they can remain anonymous if they so wish. It is also a flexible and adaptable technique. The obvious limitation is that your evaluation rests on verbal report; you may have few, if any, 'objective' measures of its success. But this is not crucial, because the success of appraisal is, like beauty, very much in the eye of the beholder(s)! If the questionnaire evaluation indicates that either party to an appraisal interview is unhappy about it, the chances of that interview producing much that is constructive are few. If, on the other hand, appraisers and appraisees generally report satisfaction with the style and outcome of the appraisal, then the scheme is probably going as well as can be hoped – no appraisal scheme can last long without such a favourable attitude from the prime consumers!

Conducting a questionnaire evaluation

What should a questionnaire on appraisal contain, and to whom should it go? Well, you could simply sit down and dream up a few questions yourself without much difficulty, but the result would reflect the way you think about appraisal and your own priorities rather than anybody else's. This is the danger of the personnel specialist devising evaluation tools in isolation. The questionnaire has to evolve out of a lengthier process than this. The first stage is to build up a pool of items (questions) based on observation of appraisals or of practice appraisal interviews, and on conversations with appraisers and appraisees. The items will reflect the perspectives of the different users of the system. Having put together a draft questionnaire, it needs to be piloted on a small sample of appraisers and their subordinates. They should complete it in relation to their most recent appraisal and then discuss the questionnaire, item by item, with whoever is devising it. The aim is to check first that the questions are clear and convey the same meaning to everyone completing them, and second that they do not appear to miss anything relevant that is seen as important to the participants generally.

What comes out of such a process is usually a questionnaire that breaks down into three main sections. The first short section deals with characteristics of the respondent and other factual data (age, sex, grade or level, amount of experience of appraisal interviews, time since the last interview). The second part covers what went on in the interview and the reactions to it (what topics were or were not discussed). The final group of questions focuses on the perceived outcomes of the appraisal and overall attitudes towards it. However, two questionnaires are needed, one for the appraisers and one for the appraisees. Not only are their concerns in appraisal different, but their accounts of the same interview can differ markedly from one another. This was the conclusion drawn from a study done in an operating division of a British multinational company.[4] A typical example of the conflicting accounts of interviews was that appraisers said they had communicated evaluations of the subordinates' weaknesses more often than the subordinates said they had received them. One is inclined to believe the subordinates more in this instance; probably the managers did not deal with weaknesses as often as they claimed, or they did so in such a roundabout way that the appraisees did not notice. This emphasises the fact that there is little point in asking the managers doing the appraisal such direct questions as 'Did you let the appraisee put his or her point of view across?', or anything else which in effect says bluntly 'Did you carry out the interview in the way you were supposed to?' The answer, not surprisingly, will always be 'Yes'. It is best to concentrate in the appraisers' questionnaire on getting their views as to what problems were encountered in doing the interviews and what the effects of the appraisal seemed to be – did the manager or the subordinate appear to get anything out of the interview? Since most of them will have done a number of appraisals, the questions will need to be framed in general terms rather than relating to a specific interview.

The appraisee's questionnaire should concentrate on such things as the extent of their participation – did they feel able to put across their own point of view? And were the things the appraisee is likely to want to have discussed actually covered? Again, the perceived outcome of the interview, in various respects, is an important element of the questionnaire. Clearly, the responses you get will not be an entirely faithful representation of what actually happened – as we noted before, this is a subjective report, and as such it will be open to distortions caused by errors of recall, defensiveness on the part of the respondent, and so on. You would not, therefore, wish to place undue reliance on the answers contained in any one questionnaire, but taking the replies of many appraisees you should get a reasonable picture of what is going on and how the system is being received. Appendices A and B present examples of appraiser and appraisee questionnaires respectively.

A word on sampling is in order here. If the organization is small, then all staff involved in appraisal can be covered. In larger set-ups, some kind of representative sampling is required. This can be done on the basis of percentage samples taken randomly from personnel records (seniority lists, payroll lists, etc.), but unless everyone is appraised at the same time and in the same way, this kind of approach can lead you into a rather time-consuming and cumbersome exercise. It is probably best to select a few representative sections of the organization and do a total survey there – trying to ensure that there is a reasonable balance of ages, sexes, grade levels and specialist and/or managerial functions.

The processing and analysis of the data once you have the questionnaires back can be done either on a computer or by hand. The former is obviously best – indeed essential – if a large number of, say, more than 200 is used. The SPSS suite of programs[5] is the most useful here though other packages will do. The extent to which facilities of this kind are available within the organization can be bought in from a computer bureau or supplied by consultants will be a major determinant of the scale of the evaluation. A lot can, however, be learned from smaller surveys, and the actual analysis of the data is straightforward enough whether it is done by hand or by computer. All that is required generally is the calculation of the responses to each question in percentages, and possibly the application of the chi-square statistic[6] to test for the significance of any differences that might be observed between the responses of particular groups (for example, between satisfaction with appraisal of sales staff compared with production staff).

One final point on the questionnaire evaluation technique is that a decision has to be taken on the timing of the exercise. If one of the aims is to find out what went on in the interview, and whether the interviews did appear to follow the training given, the questionnaire has to be sent out fairly soon after the interview has taken place, while it is still fresh in the minds of the participants. But then you find that if part of the evaluation is to assess factors such as perceived performance improvement, there has not been enough time for this to show up (or if it has, you do not know whether it is a short-term 'honeymoon' effect). There are two basic ways around this problem. The first is to stagger the sending out of questionnaires so that they arrive at varying times after the appraisal for different people – some receiving them almost immediately afterwards and some several months later. One can then make comparisons between groups and allow for this time effect. The other method is simply to use two questionnaires, one concentrating on the interview itself, and the other on perceived results, with the two being sent out on separate occasions.

Getting co-operation for evaluation studies
While monitoring the success or otherwise of an expensively-introduced appraisal system may seem eminently sensible to you and to us, it is not, alas, seen that way by everybody. Assuming that top management can be convinced of the necessity of protecting this particular investment, the next obstacle in many organizations is the staff association or trade union. There is a growing interest in appraisal on the part of the trade unions in the UK and this can generally be used in getting their co-operation. The problem is that survey methods are sometimes seen by unions as a threat – a way for management to

consult the union membership directly, thus cutting out the union and undermining part of its *raison d'être*. So the use of a questionnaire survey has to be negotiated carefully. The essential thing is to involve them right from the start, not just seeking their agreement to the study but a degree of participation as well – on deciding the appropriate content of the questionnaire, the sample to be chosen, and so on. Equal access to the final report is usually part of the deal.

The agreement of top management and of staff organizations does not of itself guarantee that the individual appraiser or appraisee who gets a questionnaire is going to fall over himself in his desire to respond. It has to be 'sold' to the participants directly. There are a number of aspects to this. A preliminary step is to make the evaluation survey known to people beforehand – through office notices, information bulletins, in-house magazines, etc. Then the questionnaires themselves need a covering letter (see Appendix C) that will strike the right tone in asking the respondent's help and will explain the purpose of the exercise and emphasize the agreement (and participation) of the unions or staff associations. If only a sample of staff will receive questionnaires, that needs explaining, including how the sample was selected. The same goes for the question of whether or not the survey is an anonymous one and, if it is not, who will see the responses and what safeguards there are on confidentiality.

The issue of anonymity and confidentiality is a particularly important one if the survey is to obtain a worthwhile response rate. And the question of who actually carries out the evaluation is mixed in with this too. An evaluation study is likely to get the best response when it assures the respondents of anonymity. However, some people never seem entirely convinced that an internally mounted exercise is genuinely anonymous; they imagine that Personnel have some fiendish trick of finding out who completed a questionnaire without it being evident to the individual involved. This argues for the use of some external agency to carry out the study. However, there may then be a problem of giving outside consultants access to personal information about staff. One way around this is to have the personnel department put a serial number on each questionnaire sent out and to put the same serial number on a sheet giving details (but not the name) of the person to whom the questionnaire has been sent. This sheet of biographical/ career details is sent to the consultant running the evaluation, and the respondents likewise return their questionnaires to the same person. By matching up the questionnaire and personal information sheet serial numbers, all the necessary information on an individual is acquired while maintaining anonymity and without breaching confidentiality. Moreover, by looking at the information sheets on those people who have not returned questionnaires one can check for any systematic and important differences between respondents and non-respondents.

How to use the evaluation data

The interpretation of data from evaluation studies can be done in such a way as to be reasonably uncomplicated. There are certain interview behaviours that are desirable, and some that are not. Similarly, there are some topics you want to be sure were raised in the interview, and others which might best have been avoided. You want to see a majority of respondents reporting positive effects from the appraisal. All of these things are readily ascertained from the results. But what is the level of positive results with which you can feel satisfied? For example, is it reasonable and realistic to expect all appraisees to have their job satisfaction increased by an appraisal interview, or perhaps half of them, or maybe just 10 per cent? Ideally, you would have some 'norms' by which to assess your results, otherwise they have to be matched up with your existing expectations which could be either too high or too low. (Incidentally, to prevent anyone turning around later on and saying 'Well, that's only what I expected anyway', try asking them to predict *beforehand* what the breakdown of the responses will be.)

There are, though, no proper 'norms' for appraisal evaluation data, but we can go part of the way towards meeting this need. A series of questionnaires developed by one of the authors[7] for use in evaluating appraisal systems in government departments in the 1970s has been used extensively in that context, and has been adopted in a number of other public and private sector organizations in the UK and overseas. While there has inevitably been some variation in the questionnaire items used to account for differences in appraisal practices and aims, many of them have been used quite consistently. There is thus a set of data for organizations with good, average and poor appraisal systems against which fresh results can be compared. It is not possible to present all of this here, but some of the most useful items for comparative purposes are shown in Table 1, and examples of the questionnaires from which they are drawn are given in Appendices A and B.

The data in Table 1 are based on studies in seven organizations – some small, some large – in both the public and private sectors. The total number of appraisees and appraisers responding in these studies was 5940 and 1332 respectively; all of the studies had acceptable response rates, most of them being very high indeed (75 per cent to 95 per cent). The highest positive outcome achieved by any one of the studies is shown in Table 1, along with the least favourable outcome on each item. Also given is the *average* of the results for all the organizations on each item. (In some cases, one or other of the organizations did not include that item in their evaluation, so this figure sometimes represents five, six or seven organizations.) Thus, Table 1 gives the highest and lowest extremes and an average for each variable.

Table 1   *Comparison of data from evaluation studies done in various organizations*

Percentage of cases in which:	Best result achieved by any organization (per cent)	Average (per cent)	Worst result achieved by any organization (per cent)
The interviewee was given some notice of the appraisal interview beforehand	99	91	67
The interviewee did some preparation for the interview	83	62	16
The interviewer spent over half an hour (on average) preparing for each interview	95	69	34
The appraisal interviews lasted more than one hour*	34	20	5
Performance weaknesses were discussed in the appraisal interview	81	54	40
Training needs were discussed	70	47	21
The appraisee reported his or her job satisfaction increased by the interview	40	30	15
The appraisee thought his or her job performance had improved (or was likely to) as a result of the appraisal	54	40	20
The appraisee was against the whole scheme	3	9	25

* It is not necessarily the case that a long interview indicates positive qualities, of course, but, in general, research shows that duration is correlated with favourability of outcome.

We have written so far about interpreting the results of evaluation against a yardstick of similar information collected elsewhere. This process may bring to light some aspects of the system that are working very well and some that are not. Where does one go from there? If various groups – trade unions and managers particularly – were involved in the discussions leading to the setting up of the scheme and in designing the evaluation study, then they have to be represented in the interpretation of the results and in deciding what should be done about them.

As far as the managers doing the appraisals are concerned, information on the way the scheme is functioning can be derived from

Group Feedback sessions. These not only serve the purpose of maintaining commitment to the scheme, but are one of the main opportunities for presenting the results of the questionnaire survey back to the people who yielded the data in the first place. In doing this, and in eliciting their reactions, a check is provided on the interpretation of the findings and more (often richer) evaluative information is gathered. So, these sessions are both a part of the process of maintaining the appraisal system, and a stage in its evaluation. This further stage is sometimes necessary to illuminate questionnaire data. For example, if you find that very little in the way of post-appraisal action is being decided on in the appraisal interviews, is this because:

1 the parties to the interview have not understood how to use the action sheet properly?

2 the appraisal system is geared too much towards assessment and the resulting defensiveness of the appraisees is blocking any attempt to agree constructive remedial action on their part?

3 the interviewers' approach is too authoritarian and prescriptive, with the result that they suggest what should be done but the appraisees are reluctant to agree?

4 there is genuinely just little action to take. Without some further probing, a diagnosis of this kind is difficult to make.

There is little point in doing evaluation if, at the end, any deficiencies of the appraisal scheme that have been identified are left uncorrected. Sometimes all that is needed is a note to appraisers, or some simple procedure to be implemented centrally. In other instances, however, more extensive corrective action is required. If the scheme has been devised and implemented properly in the first place, this is much less likely to be the case. But it does sometimes happen that, for one reason or another, the organization has just got it wrong. (Case Study 3 presents an illustration of a failed system.) The question then is whether to invest further time and money in changing the system, often entailing a modification of the appraisal forms and/or some further training, or whether to close your eyes and carry on regardless. If the latter is the answer, then the entire exercise has been a waste of time. With this in mind, it is worth gently testing the willingness to contemplate remedial increases (if the need arises) at the outset.

Earlier in the chapter, the monitoring of reporting standards was discussed, as was the need to analyse the type of action recommendations coming out of appraisals and to follow them up. Since then our attention has concentrated on questionnaire measures of the content and direct outcomes of appraisal interviews. There are, however, other aspects to the evaluation process which need mentioning, and mostly they relate to longer-term effects and the running of the system.

Some further approaches to evaluation

The impact of the appraisal system on such things as the level of manager-subordinate communication and job satisfaction may be considerable. An appraisal system is as potent a form of organization development as any you will find – and perhaps more potent than most. Its effects are likely to be particularly marked when previous appraisal arrangements have been minimal or non-existent. A study in a government department illustrates this wider picture:

The investigation[8] was carried out in two stages, the first before a new report form and system of appraisal interviews were introduced (there had previously been a form but no appraisal interview), and the second after the appraisal scheme had been running for three years. The first stage questionnaire concentrated on general attitudes to work, supervision and communications with management, while the later questionnaire presented some of the same questions again (to see if there had been any change) as well as some new ones which related to the appraisals directly.

Around 500 questionnaires were sent out to matched samples of staff, covering clerical to middle management grades in both administrative and specialist groups, on each occasion. A very high response rate was obtained, giving some degree of confidence in the findings. Comparison of the results of the first study with the second (by which time all the respondents had been given between one and four appraisals) showed that there had been a statistically significant increase in the amount of discussion taking place between managers and staff and between supervisors and staff. In line with this, the staff reported feeling much freer to talk to their managers than they had previously. To check that this was not just a more favourable response to any question asked, items had been included on which no change would have been expected following the introduction of the appraisals and, accordingly, no change was found. While this study cannot prove a cause-and-effect relationship between the introduction of the new system and the improved communications, the findings are highly suggestive of at least some link.

Similar to the questionnaire survey approach described above is the Management Development Audit devised at the Durham University Business School. This too incorporates the use of questionnaires and interviews, but is broader in its coverage, including training and career development activities as well as appraisal. Interviews are used, with senior managers, personnel, and management development and training specialists, to gather information on what is supposed to happen. The questionnaire survey is used to obtain information from managers themselves on what they perceive to be happening in actual practice. We concentrate here on findings about appraisal, drawing on audits described in *Auditing Management Development*.[9]

The audits revealed a diverse range of findings – from organizations in which there was little appraisal activity or where appraisal discussions were not held uniformly, to those where there was a high level of activity. But a high level of activity does not necessarily mean that that the appraisals are done well – for example, there may be insufficient discussion, with managers not knowing where they stand both in regard to their current performance and their future potential. In the light of our earlier comments about the need to take action on survey results, it is interesting to consider organizational responses to these problems; they were similarly diverse and included such ideas as:

- Setting objectives to the appraisal scheme, and involving line managers in this process.

- Developing better methods of assessing potential and of identifying managers' aspirations.

- Assessing performance against agreed objectives.

- Providing for managers' self-assessments as the basis of the appraisal.

- Ensuring that the results of appraisals are used, for example in decisions about training, transfer, or promotion.

Beyond appraisal, the audits revealed other problem areas, most of which ought now to come as no surprise given our earlier criticisms of training and career development. Problems included:

- Inadequate identification of training and development needs.

- Insufficient involvement of prospective trainee in decisions about training and careers.

- Poor briefing of trainee before attending course.

- Lack of follow-up after training.

- Insufficient training and development.

- Vagueness of management development policy, sometimes seen as being for an elite group.

- Lack of information about training opportunities.

- Providing opportunities for staff with potential and for those who have reached a plateau.

- Uncertainty over management skills and knowledge required in the organization.

Audits of this kind can be a particularly powerful diagnostic tool to identify areas of personnel practice which are not working as intended. This information may then be used as a basis for corrective action.

Another longer-term, but less systematic, type of evaluation – one that in many people's eyes is an acid test of the value and credence gained by the appraisal scheme – concentrates on the *use* made of it for other management purposes. We have, for example, already pointed to inadequate linkages between appraisal and training systems. What of the relationship of appraisals to promotion decisions? Do the managers making such decisions ask to see the recent appraisals of the candidates? Will they accept a shortlist of suitable individuals prepared by the personnel department on the basis of appraisal data? How willing are they to promote or reject someone for a new position against the indications provided by written appraisals? And is the content of the appraisal form accepted as it stands? Or do managers (in the line or Personnel) considering internal candidates for a position insist on ringing up existing appraisers to get 'the real picture' of the candidate? The trust that is placed in an appraisal system becomes evident without much effort by the personnel department – the trouble is that this type of feedback comes too late because, if things have gone wrong, by the time the lack of trust in the system becomes evident, too much damage has been done for anything but a very major overhaul to have any effect.

We have written a lot in this chapter about various approaches to evaluation – some of it in considerable detail. There are two main reasons for devoting so much time and space to this topic. The first is that it is an aspect of appraisal that personnel managers seem to be less well acquainted with, and it is often not covered in any depth in general personnel management texts; the evaluation of training is about all that gets a look in. The other, more basic, reason for giving the topic so much attention is that it is, we feel, nothing less than good personnel practice to evaluate appraisals. In the past it has been relatively unusual to find organizations doing it, but this may change as they strive to fulfil their equal employment opportunity obligations, which will necessitate a degree of evaluation activity.

Evaluation and equal opportunity

The sorts of evaluation activities described here, and the care and maintenance activities reviewed earlier, clearly illustrate the sorts of things that can be done. The only additional requirement is to make comparisons on the basis of sex or ethnic origins. The former comparison is likely to be quite straightforward as information about sex is recorded routinely. Looking at equal opportunities for minority groups is rather more difficult, however, as information about ethnic origins tends not to be recorded – although more and more organizations are starting to do so.[10] The issue of recording ethnic information is a highly sensitive one, involving not just the means by which the information is obtained (self-identification or other means), but also the classification scheme that is used to categorize the various ethnic groups. For more detailed advice on these points we refer the reader to relevant materials from the Commission for Racial Equality[11] and other publications such as David Wainwright's *Discrimination in Employment*.[12] Our major concern here is with approaches to evaluation, particularly those relating to appraisal.

One illustration of what can be done is found in a report of studies undertaken by the Tavistock Institute[13] which aimed to examine personnel policies from the point of view of the employment of minorities. As well as looking at appraisal, the studies examined recruitment, postings, promotion, training, and so on. With regard to appraisal, the approach taken was to look in detail at certain aspects of completed report forms and to make comparisons between minorities and whites. In so doing, the researchers found instances in which coloured clerical staff fared less well than their white counterparts. For example, in terms of aspects of performance judged to be of high job importance, coloured staff were found to receive fewer of the higher performance markings and more of the lower performance markings than did the white staff. It has to be recognized that such findings as these do not constitute evidence of racial discrimination, but there is no doubt that such ratings may place coloured staff in a disadvantageous position, given that, as we have shown, appraisal reports often tend to play a significant part in promotion decisions and sometimes in transfer decisions. Such evidence, therefore, is a signal to the organization that some action may be necessary. If, for example, coloured staff receive lower ratings than whites on oral expression, this may suggest a need for supplementary training. Sometimes though, the lower markings may be a reflection of stereotyping by the line managers who complete the appraisal forms. Examples of such stereotyping are that white manual workers learn a skill more quickly and are easier to deal with than blacks, or that West Indians are less conscientious and less organized and methodical than whites. Thus, where the lower ratings are a function of the appraiser rather than the appraisee, this perhaps points to a training need on the part of the appraiser. We feel this is an area where much appraisal training is deficient: it is not enough to warn managers against the risk of appraising minorities less favourably than whites – there needs to be more emphasis on enabling managers to recognize and overcome their personal biases.

Another interesting finding from the Tavistock studies was that where low ratings were given there tended not to be any specification of a training need. This applied to whites just as much as to coloured employees – further evidence, therefore, of the potential deficiency of the appraisal scheme for identifying training needs.

Detailed examination of appraisal forms can be carried out in the same way to compare the treatment of women with that of men. A basic question is whether women are actually included in the scheme. Given the coverage of appraisal schemes – essentially management levels – there is a strong possibility that many women will be excluded, as a preponderance of women are employed in, for example, clerical and secretarial occupations. But the attitude is that 'appraisal for women in these occupations is not worth it, is it? After all they only come to work for pin money or for company and are not interested in promotion. And the young married women will leave anyway to have kids.' These assertions are, without doubt, true for some women, but certainly not for all. Some men may also come to work for the company, but not all. It is important to recognize that such stereotyped attitudes do not apply to all individual cases and that allowing them to influence the implementation of policies can have detrimental consequences of the kind described – for example, the exclusion of women. Thus, there may be the same training need as for the appraisal of minorities – recognizing and overcoming personal biases.

Assuming that at least some women are covered by the appraisal scheme, how well do they fare when compared to men? Are the overall performance assessments of women comparable with those for men? If not, might stereotyped views of some kind be affecting the assessments? For example, there is some evidence[14] to suggest that good performance by women is sometimes attributed to luck rather than to ability unless, perhaps, it is a 'woman's' job, in which case it requires less ability and effort than a 'man's' job does. If the woman's performance was poor, on the other hand, this might be attributed to lack of ability, whereas this does not always happen with a man's poor performance – bad luck is sometimes the explanation. It is possible, of course, that lower assessments for women are accurate reflections of their actual performance, in which case there may be a need for supplementary training. Ideally, one would expect this to be revealed in the appraisal form, with a training recommendation. But, as we know, the appraisal scheme often falls down in this respect, and women can fare less well than men with fewer training needs being identified and met[15] An interesting side-point here about self-appraisal for women is that there is a tendency for them to identify weaknesses first rather than strengths, and that women are diffident about discussing performance strengths.[16]

Having looked at assessments of performance and of training needs, potential assessments made on appraisal forms (or separately) might next be scrutinized. Are the proportions of men and women identified as having potential comparable? If not, the possible reasons for the discrepancy should be examined. Stereotypes present a possible, but partial, explanation – women leave, they are not interested in promotion. Agreed, these reasons may apply to some women but, for example, some women may want to return to employment after a break to have children. Does the organization encourage reinstatement? And what about all the women in their thirties and forties? – at least some of these must have ambitions and the potential to realize those ambitions. If women do receive lower potential ratings, another possible explanation is that they truly have less potential. This might provoke one or both of two responses on the part of the organization.

The first response is that there may be a need for special training for women, which may or may not be for women only. Under-representation of women at, say, management levels is another factor to be considered in determining the organizational need for such training. Legislative requirements, as set out in the Sex Discrimination Act which provides for certain kinds of positive action, also have to be met. An illustration of single sex training for women is presented as Example 6.1 and a report[17] of a conference sponsored by the former Manpower Services Commission shows a range of approaches relevant to career development for women.

The second response is to independently confirm the appraisal judgements. A training course may be one way of doing this, but in this country it is unusual for training to be used in this way. Promotion procedures usually incorporate a number of elements – probably an interview or two as well as the appraisal – and these may serve as a check on the appraisal ratings. But there are difficulties here. If the appraisals are used as a first sift before candidates are considered at an interview or by some other means, then it is possible that some women will be screened out at this stage. (This same point applies to members of minority groups as well.) So, the organization must examine the operation of its promotion procedures at this point.

Another difficulty is that it cannot be assumed that an interview is free from bias. Therefore, training for interviewers should deal with the issue of discrimination – in specific terms, such as the type of question to be avoided, rather than in general terms, such as 'be careful to avoid discrimination on the grounds of sex and race'. Written guidance material may also help. Another means of confirming line managers' judgements of potential is through the use of assessment centres (see earlier chapters) – some American evidence suggests that these may represent a less discriminatory approach to the assessment of potential than do the more traditional methods.

Finally, what about evaluation in the eyes of the law? We have already had instances in which appraisal forms have been called as evidence in race and sex discrimination cases. What has not yet happened – although we believe that it will – is for appraisal forms to receive the

Example 6.1   *An illustration of women-only training*

This Example[18] describes a one-week course entitled 'Developing Skills for Women in Middle Management'; it is one of the few (though increasing in number) courses for women only. The general aims of the course are:

'To help women prepare for careers in middle management, increasing their level of competence by the acquisition and development of managerial skills.'

The main topics dealt with on each day are as follows:

Day 1:   Career planning
Day 2:   Assertiveness techniques
Day 3:   Personal effectiveness in management
Day 4:   Organizational processes
Day 5:   Managing work and family life
            Action planning

The course work is mostly carried out in small groups – exercises with discussion and feedback on behaviour. There are some plenary sessions which are used primarily to give information on specific topics and to introduce and close discussion.

End-of-course reaction evaluation shows participants reporting benefits of the following kinds:

- Better self-awareness – feelings and behaviour, and how to behave assertively.

- Boosted morale.

- Better sense of career direction (including personal life) and a more positive attitude (related to self-confidence).

- Clearer understanding of job and role within the organization.

- Reassurance through the sharing of experience – that others have similar problems.

The course, being for women only, was supported enthusiastically; it was also felt that this provided a more supportive atmosphere which enhanced learning.

same judicial scrutiny as has happened in the United States. There, the stronger equal employment opportunity legislation embraces performance appraisals, because they constitute a 'selection procedure' used in various 'employment decisions', such as decisions about promotion, transfer or dismissal. If under these circumstances there is adverse impact on a race, sex, or ethnic group, the performance appraisal system must meet the specified requirements for job relatedness, that is the appraisal system must demonstrably be a valid measure of job performance. Failure to do this can lead the employer into difficulties – such as incurring heavy financial penalties if the case is won by the party alleging discrimination. On the basis of a number of reviews[19] of cases in which performance appraisals have featured, it is possible to identify a number of deficiencies in appraisal schemes which may place them at risk as valid measures.

The corrective actions include the sorts of things we have described already. Thus, the content of the appraisal must be developed through job analysis so as to be able to demonstrate the validity, or job-relatedness, of the scheme. All the significant performance dimensions of the job must be represented appropriately. Where rating scales are used these should not be of vague or subjective factors. The appraisers must be in a position to observe the performance that they are to assess. Some degree of subjectivity in appraisals is inevitable, but care needs to be taken to minimize the risk of bias: this therefore reinforces the need for training, clear written instructions and a statement of equal employment opportunity policy. And, finally, the appraisal system should be formal and standardized.

Summary

When appraisal and career development schemes are put into operation, they need careful monitoring and control to maintain standards. Various steps can be taken to this end, including the scrutinizing of the content of written reports, the follow-up of action recommendations arising from appraisals, and the appraising of managers on the quality of their own appraisal and development of subordinates. Appraisal systems need evaluating so that problems can be identified early. One of the most effective ways of doing this is by a questionnaire survey of appraisers and appraisees. But in setting up an evaluation study of this kind it is important to involve both top management and trade unions. Feeding back the findings to the participants and acting on any deficiencies identified in the study is vital. Such an approach can be used to assess the longer-term impact of appraisal, training and career development policies. Another tell-tale sign of the effectiveness of an appraisal system is the trust put in it by management when making decisions on matters like promotion. Finally, evaluation of appraisal and development practices is important in terms of its potential to identify whether they are providing equality of opportunity for both sexes and for ethnic minorities.

References

1   D.L. DeVries, M.W. McCall, Jr., 'Performance appraisal: Is it tax time again?', paper presented at a conference on 'Managerial Performance Feedback: Appraisals and Alternatives', at the Center for Creative Leadership, Greensboro, North Carolina (1976).

2   F.A. Heller, 'Group feedback analysis: a method of field research', *Psychological Bulletin*, **72** (1969) pp. 108–17.

3   H. Coolican, *Research Methods and Statistics in Psychology* (Hodder and Stoughton 1990).

4   C. Sofer and M. Tuchman, 'Appraisal interviews and the structure of colleague relations', *Sociological Review*, **8** (1970) pp. 365–92.

5   A. Bryman and D. Cramer, *Quantitative Data Analysis for Social Scientists* (Routledge 1990).

6   H. Coolican, *Research Methods and Statistics in Psychology*.

7   C. Fletcher, 'An evaluation study of Job Appraisal Reviews', *Management Services in Government*, **28** (1973) pp. 188–95.
    C. Fletcher, *Job Appraisal Reviews in the Civil Service Department*, BSRD Report No. 20 (Civil Service Department 1974).
    C. Fletcher, *An Appraisal of Appraisals: Job Evaluation Review Study in the Property Services Agency*, BSRD Report No. 33 (Civil Service Department 1976).

8   S.V. Dulewicz, C. Fletcher and J. Walker, 'Job Appraisal Reviews three years on', *Management Services in Government*, 31(1976), pp. 134–43.

9   M. Easterby-Smith, E. Braiden and D. Ashton, *Auditing Management Development* (Gower 1980).

10 Organizations which record ethnic origins include Ford, British Airways.

11 For example, Commission for Racial Equality, *Why Keep Ethnic Records?* (Commission for Racial Equality 1980).
    See also, The British Psychological Society & the Runnymede Trust, *Discriminating Fairly* (The British Psychological Society & The Runnymede Trust 1980).

12 D. Wainwright, *Discrimination in Employment* (Associated Business Press 1979).

13 Civil Service Department, *Application of Race Relations Policy in the Civil Service* (HMSO 1978).

14 V.F. Nieva and B.A. Gutek, 'Sex effects on evaluation', *Academy of Management Review*, **5** (1980), pp. 267–76.

15 Ashridge Management College, *Employee Potential: issues in the development of women* (Institute of Personnel Management 1980).

16 ibid.

17 C.L. Cooper, *Practical approaches to women's career development* (Manpower Services Commission 1982).

18 R.S. Williams and P. Glucklich, *Developing Skills for Women in Middle Management: First Report on Course Evaluation* (Management and Personnel Office 1982).

19 W.H. Holley and H.S. Feild, 'Will your performance approval system hold up in court?', *Personnel*, **59** (1982), pp. 59–64.
    B.R. Nathan and W.F. Cascio, 'Introduction. Technical and Legal Standards', in R.A. Berk (ed.), *Performance Assessment* (Johns Hopkins University Press 1986).

7
Persisting issues

Throughout the earlier chapters we have touched on issues which have endured for years, in some cases decades, and which seem likely to persist for the foreseeable future. These include disclosure and the effects of performance feedback, participation and self-appraisal, accuracy in appraisal, the use of assessment centres, and the role of the line manager in development. The purpose of this chapter is to look again at these issues and the questions they raise. By their very nature, it is difficult to offer any definitive answers. However, readers can review the evidence presented here and make up their own minds as to whether they agree with our interpretation of it. The number of references cited in bringing forward the evidence may give this chapter a rather academic feel at times – but these are certainly not just academic questions: they are central to the policy and practice of appraisal.

Accuracy in appraisal

Does accuracy just depend on what is appraised and the method used? Without doubt the first step on the road to getting accuracy in performance appraisal is to have a clear specification of the performance to be assessed. This applies whatever approach to appraisal one adopts. A results- or objectives-based approach might, by its very nature, be expected to embody a statement of the performance required. An approach using rating scales, however, needs to be developed through job analysis studies. As to the methods themselves, it is clear that no one method is especially superior to another. But then, quite apart from content and method, other factors influence the accuracy of performance appraisals.

What other factors affect accuracy?
The 'what' and the 'how' are features of performance appraisal systems over which organizations can have a high degree of control, and organizations consequently believe that control over these leads to a high degree of accuracy. The other factors which bear on accuracy are, by

contrast, much harder to control, not the least because there are so many.

- People vary considerably in their ability and motivation to evaluate accurately the behaviour of others. Due to lack of training in how to observe subordinate behaviour, or lack of ability to do so, the immediate supervisor may not be qualified to act as appraiser.
- The experience of the appraiser (as an appraiser) may affect the quality of appraisal.
- In many instances the immediate supervisor may lack the first-hand information required to make valid assessments. Thus, physical distance from the subordinate, unfamiliarity with the job requirements or duties, or lack of opportunities to observe the subordinate's work can result in inaccurate assessments.
- Different appraisers may apply different standards of judgement in making their assessments. As well as this individual variation, the position of the appraiser – immediate superior or 'grandfather' – the type of job held by the appraiser, or the sex or race of the appraiser, may influence ratings.
- Supervisors may feel that if they rate their subordinates unfavourably this will reflect poorly on them as supervisors. The corollary of this is that 'good' assessments will reflect favourably.
- Supervisors may be influenced by the purposes to which appraisals are put. They may fear the consequences of disclosure. They may rate leniently in the belief that this will improve their subordinates' chances of promotion.
- The nature and quality of the appraisee's job or the race or sex of the appraisee may influence the assessments.

Given that there are so many factors involved it is only to be expected that there is inaccuracy in appraisals. The conclusion we draw is that organizations should accept that this will be so and therefore decrease their reliance on appraisals for administrative purposes, such as promotion decisions. But if appraisals are used in this way they should be supplemented by other methods having a greater demonstrated validity.

Performance feedback and disclosure

Are the effects of giving performance feedback inevitably bad? In the previous section we commented that supervisors may fear negative consequences from the disclosure of performance appraisals. More generally, we have had cause, in earlier chapters, to mention the debate on the functions of appraisal and particularly on the alleged incompatibility of the evaluating and helping roles in appraisal. Is it an inevitable consequence of relaying unfavourable comments on the subordinate's performance that he or she becomes defensive and unwilling to accept or implement subsequent suggestions on how to improve?

Following the publication of the work done by Herbert Meyer and his colleagues[1] in the General Electric Company during the 1960s, this certainly became the orthodox belief. But careful reading of the reports on this work reveals that, on average, appraisees received no less than thirteen criticisms in each interview! Faced with such a tirade it is small wonder that they reacted somewhat less than positively. Studies that have been done since have produced a variety of conclusions, some finding no effect at all,[2] some finding a mixture of effects (positive on the perceived utility of appraisal, none on resulting satisfaction, and a detrimental effect with younger appraisees),[3] and some finding almost entirely positive effects[4]. Overall, the weight of evidence suggests that criticism does *not* normally bring about an adverse effect on appraisal, although whether it achieves any beneficial effect depends heavily on a series of other factors.

What are the conditions necessary for constructive and effective feedback?

The *amount* of critical feedback conveyed is important. Most appraisees appear to be able to deal constructively with criticism of two aspects of their performance, but not with more than that in any one appraisal.[5] Furthermore, any *critical comment should be balanced with recognition of work done well* or at least competently[6] to get the best reaction. *The degree of self-review and participation* by the appraisee is a vital factor, as will be seen when this is discussed in the next section. Partly related to this is *the way the feedback is handled* by the appraiser[7] – *a problem-solving orientation* that focuses on job difficulties rather than on the personal characteristics of the individual is the most effective one generally[8] – though of course skill in conducting a successful appraisal does not just boil down to the adoption of this or any other approach. Another factor is the *extent to which other sources of feedback are available* to the individual[9] – if he or she gets plenty of indication of how he or she is performing from the nature of the work itself (rarely the case in managerial jobs) or from a conscientious supervisor who lets him or her know on a day-to-day basis (often not the case either),[10] then more of the same in an appraisal may, if it is allowed to, become little more than repetition, and be superfluous at best. And finally, as far as the conditions determining the use of feedback are concerned, the *existing relationship between the manager and subordinate* cannot be over-emphasized – not just the amount of day-to-day feedback provided, but the whole style practised by the manager, the amount of communication between the two parties generally, and so on.[11]

Infrequent contact and poor relationships are unlikely to result in critical assessments being accepted as valid or fair.

Only by taking into account all the above factors can you predict whether giving performance feedback in appraisal interviews is likely to help or hinder. Even then, given favourable conditions, it *may* contribute to some aims of appraisal but not to others (particularly appraisee satisfaction).[12] What does seem wise is to keep the emphasis on the performance of the job itself and, where there are problems or deficiencies in this, to set goals relating to these for the individual to achieve, rather than to fall back on general exhortations to improve. Goal-setting is a technique with proven effectiveness across a range of situations,[13] and, combined with performance feedback, probably offers the best approach to appraisal interviewing.[14]

If you don't show the form, can appraisees get a clear picture of where they stand?

The discussion so far has centred on the merits of identifying strengths and weaknesses in a subordinate's performance in an interview, and presumably that interview should be based on a written appraisal report. When the report is closed – that is, when the appraisee is not allowed to see the contents – then the appraiser has the choice of whether to discuss with the subordinate what weaknesses might be noted in it. It may be that he is supposed to give feedback of this kind, but that of course does not guarantee that he will. There is no doubt that, faced with a situation of this kind, many appraisers fight shy of bringing up any unsatisfactory aspects of job performance.[15] There is some evidence, however, to show that, over time and as both parties get more accustomed to the appraisal interview and more skilled in using it, many appraisees are able to get an increasingly accurate impression of how they stand on performance. Fletcher[16] found that after one appraisal interview 52 per cent of appraisees had a correct impression of their overall performance rating. (This was in a 'closed' reporting system where the individual was supposed to be given feedback on performance without any actual ratings being disclosed.) After three interviews 79 per cent had a correct impression; see Figure 4. But there was no parallel finding for discussion of promotion prospects, where this took place. There was a consistent tendency for appraisees to come away from the interview with an over-optimistic idea of their assessment on this, suggesting that the appraisers had been sufficiently vague in what they had said for the appraisees to read into it what they had wanted.

What are the effects of 'open' reporting on standards of assessment?

This kind of opportunity to evade awkward issues either disappears or takes on a new form under 'open' appraisal, where some or all of what is

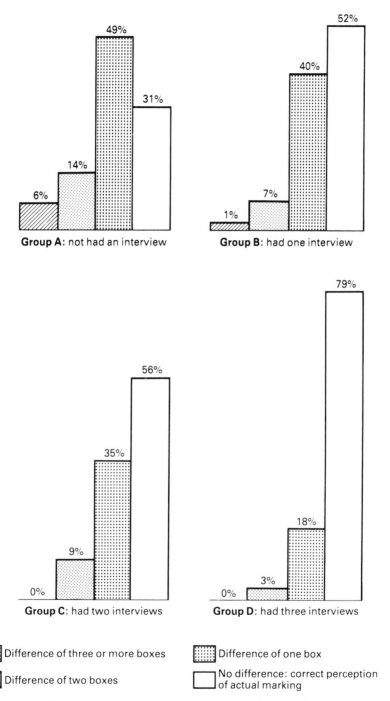

Figure 4 *Comparison of perceived with actual overall performance markings.*

written about individuals is disclosed to them – a growing practice as we noted in Chapter 2. The great fear which organizations running 'closed' appraisal schemes have is that, if they were to make them open, those appraisers who formerly held interviews that skirted round the less positive aspects of the report would just not put anything unfavourable on the report at all. Either they would inflate all the ratings so that nothing would be indicated as unsatisfactory, or they would write bland reports that communicated little of any use, or both.

Despite this worry, which particularly concerns organizations which place any reliance on appraisal reports in making promotion decisions, many companies have instituted 'open' appraisal schemes, both in the UK and abroad.[17] Have the fears over the effects of 'open' reporting been justified? A study by Walker *et al*[18] in the UK set out to find the answer to this. They reported that most of the organizations with open appraisal were satisfied with the standards of assessment achieved. Some had noted a deterioration of standards at first, followed by improvement after further training or counselling of the managers concerned. In two organizations with completely open appraisals an inflation of rating standards was said to have occurred. In those organizations where performance markings were seen by the appraisee, but where ratings of potential remained undisclosed, there were fewer problems – in fact, three organizations actually felt that the standard of reporting on present performance had improved, as appraisers took extra care that they had evidence to justify their assessments. So, opinions and experiences of the effects of disclosure on the quality of appraisal differed widely, but the general impression was that it *may* lead to a deterioriation in the quality but that it certainly does not do so in the majority of instances. The study also found that organizations which operated open appraisal procedures were generally as likely to use them in promotion and pay decisions as were those running closed appraisals.

The implications of the Walker *et al* study would seem to be that appraisers are increasingly facing up to the difficulties of giving feedback one way or another. There is little to indicate how well they are doing it, from the point of view of getting a positive reaction from their appraisees. Given all the conditions needed for this, one suspects that not a few are finding it all very difficult. The move towards open appraisal has, however, been paralleled by another trend which is perhaps an inevitable consequence of it and which also offers some help in the tricky business of reviewing subordinates' performance. This is the growing use of, and interest in, subordinate participation in the appraisal process.

Participation and self-appraisal

What do we mean by participation in appraisal and what are its effects?

Any appraisal system that involves an interview between a manager and a subordinate entails some degree of overt participation by the latter, though the appraisee's part may vary greatly according to the style of the interviewer. The extent of a subordinate's participation in an interview and the effect it exerts have been the subject of quite a lot of research over a long period,[19] but much of it is beset with methodological weaknesses and vague definitions of what participation actually involves.[20] Almost without exception, this research indicates that participation by the appraisee is positively correlated with favourable outcomes from appraisal interviews – greater satisfaction, more goal achievement, etc. The consistency of this finding makes it hard to argue with, the shortcomings of individual studies notwithstanding. But what does participation mean? Well, not just the amount the appraisees talk[21] – what they say is more important than the amount. Being asked for views on the job and its problems, on how to overcome them, on the goals for the next year and how progress is to be assessed, are all elements of participation, but they are of themselves worth little unless there is a genuine response from the appraiser – that is, a willingness to listen and to act on the subordinate's ideas. Only when the appraisee experiences what Greller[22] calls 'ownership' of the appraisal, seeing it as a joint exercise, does the participation become real and constructive. However, one cannot but help wondering, once again, just how much the degree of participation, whatever way it is defined, and the reaction to it depend on the existing relationship between the parties to the appraisal and, particularly, on the style of the manager,[23] for example, one study[24] showed that authoritarian-style managers were less likely to hold appraisal interviews at all!

Does self-appraisal really work?

Participation in an interview is one thing, but participation in writing the report is quite another. It can range from simply being allowed to write brief comments on the appraisal given, to full self-appraisal. A further variant is for the appraisee to complete a self-review form before the appraisal interview. In a sense, it is impossible to prevent self-appraisal, whatever system you operate, because people are always going to have their own views on how well they are performing, and the appraiser's opinions are going to be received against this background. That is where the problem comes in. Herbert Meyer[25] asked one group of staff in the General Electric Company to compare their own performance with that of others in similar jobs at about the same salary level; he found that, on average, each individual felt he or she was performing better than three-quarters of his or her peers were! This finding held for high, middle and lower level staff, with the more senior group being most prone to over-rating their performance. As Meyer points out, this is going to be a source of trouble when an appraiser who is genuinely required to produce some kind of reasonable distribution of ratings has to confront the individual with his or her own view on how well the job has been done. And, indeed, self-appraisals are often found to be more lenient (favourable) than are supervisors' assessments.[26]

Yet again, caution has to be exercised in drawing conclusions from the research findings. To be sure, leniency effects in self-appraisal *are* shown, but a number of factors contribute to this and they have important implications for the practical use of this approach. First, many of the research studies are just that – research studies. Meyer[27] reports that when subordinates are asked to prepare self-appraisal for real appraisal interviews, they are much more modest, possibly because modesty is a valued attribute in our culture, whereas blowing one's own trumpet is frowned upon. The type of ratings make a big difference too, and there is some evidence to suggest that when the individual's self-assessment is anchored on behavioural observation (rather than general ratings of performance qualities) there is much greater objectivity.[28] The context of the appraisal plays a part, because if pay is linked to the ratings given, then this will increase leniency effects (as it makes any other aspect of the appraisal more difficult, too). And, lastly, there are various more technical reasons for thinking that the validity of self-appraisals could be further improved.[29] So, the final picture may not be so bad – perhaps people can be encouraged to make realistic self-appraisals when comparing themselves to other people. There is clearly one type of self-appraisal which holds great promise. This is when the individual is asked to assess different aspects of his or her job performance *relative to one another*, rather than against the performance of peers. The evidence here shows that subordinates' judgements of this kind are more discriminating (less 'halo' effect) than are those of their supervisors, and that appraisals based on such self-assessments can be extremely effective.[30] Such appraisals become more development-centred, concentrating on remedying (relative) weaknesses and capitalizing on strengths. The role that the subordinate has played in identifying these increases his willingness to implement action steps arising out of them. This has been realized by practitioners of the assessment centre approach, who are now increasingly using guided self-assessment as their main approach in those assessment centres run for training and development purposes – they find that self-assessment by the participants is the best (some say the only) way to ensure that follow-up action takes place.[31] Interestingly, Meyer has found that subordinate-prepared appraisals work very well with poor performers, but less well – unsurprisingly – with authoritarian managers or where there is a dependent relationship between subordinate and manager.

Should *you* use self-appraisal?

In organizations which do not see establishing comparability as one of the functions of appraisal, and in those where there is less need for overall ratings of performance or potential, the self-appraisal approach seems to have a lot to offer. There will be those individuals who take to it less well, but that can be taken as another reason for using it, because dependent subordinates and authoritarian managers are probably not, in general, good for the organization, and an appraisal system that tries to shake them out of those styles may be beneficial in a wider sense. However, these people and others may need some help in adapting to self-appraisal, which is not surprising: as Heron[32] has pointed out, our educational institutions do not equip people with either the expectations or the skills of self-appraisal – assessment is something that is handed down from above throughout schooling (and that, perhaps, is the root of some of the defensive reactions to appraisal). Just as we need to train people in the assessment of others, we need to train them in the assessment of themselves. How many of the problems of self-appraisal arise from the fact that this is very seldom done?

Where the organization does use appraisal as a means of comparing people and possibly of rewarding them, an element of self-review still seems worthwhile. This can be done by adopting a multi-source appraisal, such as that operated in one of the companies of the Gulf Oil Group, where superiors, subordinates, peers and the appraisee all contributed to the assessment.[32] Alternatively, and less ambitiously, the procedure recommended by Teel[34] has some merit. In this, the appraiser and appraisee independently complete a report form before the interview takes place. These are compared in the interview, and disparities in ratings are dealt with like this: if there is only a one-point difference, the higher rating is agreed upon; while a two-point difference is the subject of an in-depth discussion to diagnose the reasons for it. Finally, the lowest level of self-appraisal that might be incorporated into a system would be on the lines of the 'Interview Preparation Form' used by the Civil Service since the early 1970s. This invited the appraisee to identify, amongst other things, what he had done least well in the period under review, and what he could do to improve performance in the year ahead. Research showed that the amount of use made of this form was related to the success of the appraisal interview,[35] thus demonstrating the value of even a low level of self-appraisal.

More recently we have seen another variant of self-appraisal gaining ground; this is self-appraisal as a basis for career planning. The vehicles used to encourage this type of self-appraisal include counselling (by someone other than the line manager), workbooks and workshops. Some self-report evaluations are available, principally about workshops, and this evidence provides encouragement for the further use of self-assessment activities in career development. We believe that there will be increasing use of such methods in the future, a point we shall develop in the next chapter.

The use of assessment centres

The assessment centre (AC) method and its deployment have been described elsewhere (Chapter 4), but there is a formidable number of questions raised by this approach to assessment. We will try to deal with the main ones below.

Are they effective? Do they really measure potential?

Studies of the validity of AC ratings of potential,[36] which have tested out predictions made by the assessors against measures of subsequent career success for up to thirty years,[37] give strong support to the use of the technique. The judgements made by this method do seem to be superior to those produced by any other single assessment technique. But does the AC truly measure aptitude and ability rather than just other characteristics of an individual, such as previous work experience or educational level? The use of exercises to simulate work situations and tasks (business games, committee and letter-writing exercises and so forth), in particular, raises the possibility that individuals who have been exposed to positions where they encountered some or all of these kinds of tasks in real life might be at an advantage in an AC. A study in a telecommunications company by Dulewicz and Fletcher[38] looked at the relationship between previous experience and background characteristics of participants and their performance at an AC. Specifically, they examined the participants' functional specialisms (the area of the company's operations in which they had spent most or all of their careers – manufacturing, technical, finance, etc.) and their experience of the kind of tasks presented in the AC. The results showed that the participants' specialism had no influence at all on either the overall rating of potential received at the end of the AC or on their performance in any particular exercise. The same was true, with one exception, of the participants' previous experience of the tasks. The one instance where a relationship was found was that having previously been involved in business planning activity positively influenced performance in an exercise requiring the individual to make a business plan presentation to the assessors. This study and its findings might seem to run contrary to common sense; after all, people who have been used to committees, for example, could reasonably be expected to handle them better than those who had not. Is it that simulation exercises of this sort do not accurately mirror what happens in real life? Well, the evidence available (more of which would be welcome) indicates that they do,[39] people who do well in such exercises tend to do well in comparable 'real' situations. The fact of the matter is that experience alone is no guarantee of good performance. Young managers may frequently attend committees, have to deal with all sorts of problems in their in-tray, draft difficult letters, and so on but, in the nature of managerial work, they may get little feedback on how well they are doing – particularly if their own managers are not very conscientious on this aspect of their responsibilities. Without such feedback and without knowledge of results, little effective learning can take place. Consequently, when individuals encounter simulation exercises in ACs, their performance depends more on their verbal ability and adequate intelligence than on specific knowledge and technique. So these exercises might be viewed as assessing the person's capacity for new learning and adaptation – surely of vital importance in an increasingly fast-changing environment. Incidentally, the study described also found that educational level as such was not related to performance in an AC exercise, but intelligence was.

Are ACs cost-effective? Could it all be achieved more simply and cheaply?

It has been suggested[40] that a combination of, say, a good performance appraisal system and the use of psychological tests might predict future managerial success at least as well as an AC can, and possibly at a fraction of the time and money. No definitive answer can be given to this yet, but on present knowledge it is unlikely that quick and cheap short-cuts of this kind will work as satisfactorily as an AC. As far as performance appraisal is concerned, there are at least two limiting factors. One is that performance at a lower organizational level is not a good predictor of performance at higher levels (though without other techniques it is frequently all one has to go on). The other is that the appraisers assessing long-term potential are usually being asked to make judgements about suitability to perform at a level that they themselves have not reached and thus not experienced directly.

With regard to intelligence tests, it has been found[41] that they do make a valuable contribution to AC judgements, but are less influential in assessors' decisions than are simulation exercises, and probably rightly so. Huck concludes that, beyond a certain level of intelligence, interpersonal and administrative skills are more important determinants of managerial effectiveness. There is some evidence for this view: for example, Ghiselli[42] has produced findings which seem to imply that performance as a manager is related curvilinearly to intelligence (that is, those with moderate to high intelligence do best, and those with very low or very high intelligence do less well). Also, Gill[43] suggested, from a study of the 'In-Tray' exercise, that the ability to learn decision-making skills may be related less to intelligence than to other human attributes and that, consequently, intelligence may be over-emphasized in assessing managerial potential – it helps determine the ability to learn rather than the level of achievement. All of this argues for the use of tests as a device to screen out those at the bottom end of the ability range, who would find the material of exercises in a management AC too complex, rather than as a replacement for the AC procedure as a whole. This would cut the cost of the AC procedure overall, by reducing both the number of centres and the failure rate. Something similar can be said of performance appraisal reports – they are a valuable aid for selecting those who are good prospects for attending an AC.

Other methods do not, it appears, offer an effective alternative to the use of ACs in identifying potential. But they are undeniably *cheaper*. The costs of ACs vary tremendously according to the procedure used – for a detailed consideration the reader is referred to Stewart and Stewart.[44] Whether an organization is willing to pay the extra price for the increased effectiveness of the AC approach tells you more about the organization and its beliefs in management development than it does about the 'cost-effectiveness' of ACs in any absolute sense. Indeed, it is difficult to see how one can apply such a concept in this context – how, for example, can one compute the benefits of the post-AC development counselling of the participants, or of the improvement in management skills the assessors derive from being properly trained in observation and assessment techniques as part of their preparation for serving on ACs?

What are the effects of ACs on the candidates? How can ACs be operated to maximize beneficial effects?

There is quite a lot of evidence from many countries showing that the attitudes of the participants to the AC are generally very favourable, at least immediately after the event.[45] Rather less satisfaction has been shown with the feedback of the AC findings given later and the use made of them in career development, though one UK study[46] found strongly positive reactions to this too. Of more concern, perhaps, is the longer-term effect of the AC outcome on candidates, and here there is little evidence. Where such centres are used for differentiating between those who have high development potential and those who don't, what happens to the self-perceptions of the candidates when they learn of the assessment on them? There may be a danger of creating 'crown princes' and premature failures, and, in both cases, of producing a self-fulfilling prophecy. This is particularly dangerous in the case of individuals not judged to have high potential. The organization may tend to write them off prematurely, and the individuals themselves may do likewise.[47] The effect of such 'failure' on a person's self-esteem could be very damaging, and considerable skill is needed in the feedback counselling to try to avoid this, or at least to minimize it.

The individuals' reactions to the AC process bear on how to use ACs to the best effect. The trend has been increasingly towards running them for development and training purposes rather than for selection and identification of potential. But for this to succeed there has to be a willingness on the part of the candidates to accept the assessor's judgements and to implement the development steps implied. As far as ACs are concerned, the effects of the provision of feedback have not been closely studied but, as we saw in an earlier section, it is an issue which has bounced backwards and forwards in appraisal literature for years.

The role of the line manager in employee development: crucial to success or failure

What is the role of the line manager?

At various points we have touched on the role of the line manager in training and development. Line managers have a part to play in identifying training and development needs, either at appraisal time or at other times during the year. They also have a part to play in meeting those needs – through coaching, nominations for off-the-job training activities, special assignments, job redesign, contributing to training courses, and in various other ways. Whether, or how well, line managers perform their role is quite another matter, however.

Do line managers know what their training and development responsibilities are?

It is possible that line managers fail to fully recognize or accept that they have responsibilities in this area – this is a particular risk in organizations where there is strong central control over training. It is therefore up to the top management of organizations to show that training and development are responsibilities shared by line management. And it is not sufficient to give a general statement (for example, to identify needs, help meet needs, etc.); it is necessary also to show how the line manager's responsibilities relate to those of others, for instance training specialists, and to show the extent of line managers' responsibilities. For example, if managers are expected to counsel their subordinates, is such counselling to be restricted to an individual's particular job or to cover career development more broadly? We shall elaborate on these points below, but for the present we shall comment on ways in which line managers can be made aware of their training and development responsibilities.

Policy statements and the like may be one way of helping to achieve this, but demonstrable commitment by top management is even more important. If senior management can be shown to be getting involved in training and development (see Examples 4.4 and 4.8), then this presents a good model to be followed at middle and junior levels. Another means that can be adopted to show line managers that training and development responsibilities are important is, as we have advocated earlier, to include the exercise of these responsibilities in their performance appraisal – some American organizations do this. Such a measure may do something to encourage managers to find ways of overcoming the pressure to ensure that the work gets done, which might otherwise deter them from devoting time to employee development. These same pressures may also lead managers to hold back subordinates from development activities, a tendency that may be reinforced if managers are unable to see the benefits of training and development. This is a problem which some of the more innovative training programmes (see Example 4.5) are trying to overcome.

Do line managers have the requisite knowledge and skills?
As to the problem of line managers being ill-equipped for employee development, several aspects may be identified. Line managers may not know how to identify training needs, although guidance materials may be provided to help managers with this. Line managers may not know how needs, once identified, can be met. Partly, this may be because of lack of knowledge or information – the managers may not know what options are available; partly, it may be a matter of lack of skill in, for example, coaching or counselling.

One would hope that managers would try to overcome the problem of lack of information by going to the appropriate specialists in training or personnel. But, as we saw in an earlier chapter, line managers may be unsure of what help they can get from the specialists, particularly concerning individual cases. Arguably, the responsibility here rests with the specialists to make clear what they are actually able to provide to the line managers.

Lack of skill can be overcome by various means. Written guidance is one means but the adequacy of this alone is questionable. Formal training may be more appropriate so as to give an opportunity to practice and to receive feedback. Training in appraisal interviewing is one possibility, but relatively few organizations provide adequate training.

Also, one might wonder to what extent managers generalize this training in appraisal interviewing *per se* to other similar purposes in their jobs, such as setting performance standards or giving feedback.

Training in coaching skills attracted considerable interest a few years ago as a result of an initiative on the part of the Manpower Services Commission. More recently, interest in counselling has increased and there now exist several training programmes in work-related counselling skills. Such courses are appropriate for line managers, training and personnel specialists, and for any others who have some counselling responsibilities.

What knowledge and skills do managers need for training and development?

In a somewhat generalized way we are arguing that line managers need knowledge/information and skill both to identify training and development needs and to determine how they can be met. Is it possible to be more specific about the sort of information that is needed? And how exactly should managers use the skills which we have suggested they need? To a large extent, answers to these questions depend on how broadly the managers' training and development responsibilities are defined. Consider, for example, career planning. Some practitioners[48] maintain that the basis of career planning should be the individual's current job: 'If career information focuses on personal development, work content and job importance rather than promotability, potential and career ladders, career planning can help to create more realistic expectations and help minimize career dissatisfaction.' Arguably, this is a narrow view of career planning, but it is one which suits today's climate of reduced advancement opportunities. Thus, there certainly is a part to be played by the line manager. This might be in the context of the appraisal scheme – by concentrating planning and development on the present job – but not necessarily exclusively so. Other ways in which line managers might be expected to help with this kind of planning and development include: providing challenging job opportunities, for example, through work planning or job redesign or, more broadly, through special assignments or job rotation (if the line manager's span of command allows for this); coaching (as in directly helping a subordinate to overcome a weakness in performance); giving feedback; and goal-setting and setting standards of performance. Also, there are specific activities which the manager can undertake in helping to relate off-the job activities to the individual's current job. For example, it is common for the manager to be responsible for nominating subordinates to attend off-the-job courses. Before attending the programme the subordinate and manager could usefully discuss why the subordinate is taking part and what is to be gained from it. When the subordinate returns, the manager might at the least carry out a debriefing discussion, but more is required of the manager if what has been learned from the course is to be transferred to the job. Thus, the manager is responsible for providing a supportive and encouraging climate to show that attendance was worthwhile and to allow the subordinate the opportunity to put newly acquired skills and knowledge into practice. Beyond this, some organizations involve line managers in the design and running of courses.

For many organizations and individuals, though, career planning is still about 'promotability, potential and career ladders'. But if line managers are poorly equipped to help with development related to the present job they are even less well equipped to help with planning and development in this broader sense. To the extent that the present job is a basis for longer-term career planning, the line manager should make a contribution here, for example, counselling about strengths and weaknesses in performance. But this longer-term career planning and development raises a whole host of other practical issues which may present difficulties for the manager. The individual may be grappling with conflicts between career, personal and family goals. Is the line manager the most appropriate person to counsel the individual confronting these concerns? Or should it be the personnel manager? An internal professional counsellor? Or an external professional? As we saw in an earlier chapter, there are no easy answers to these questions, but it is not hard to argue that the role of the line manager may be a limited one in this context, if only because of lack of information about other career opportunities within the organization. Managers may well lack knowledge of the skills and abilities and suchlike required in fields of work other than those which they have experienced personally. Given that many career systems encourage development within functional specialisms, it is highly likely that the manager's knowledge of other fields will be quite rudimentary. Managers may also be unaware of the chances, in numerical terms, of an individual getting promoted. The fact that there are gaps in managers' knowledge clearly limits their career counselling role; more generally, these gaps point to a need for this kind of information to be generated and made available to all those who have an interest in career planning and development. Quite apart from all this, the advancement-orientated view of career development is no longer particularly meaningful for the majority of employees in the climate of the 1980s when organizational contraction is the norm.

Under such circumstances the prospects for promotion are much reduced and there is, therefore, much to be said for concentrating planning and development on the present job and other jobs at the same organizational level.

Summary

Throughout the history of appraisal and development schemes it is possible to identify many issues which have persistently taxed those involved in designing and operating such schemes. Five of these persisting issues are identified here and looked at in the light of relevant research evidence. The first is the question of accuracy in appraisal, and the numerous factors which bear on it. Second, performance feedback and disclosure are discussed with particular reference to the conditions necessary for constructive and effective feedback and the effects of openness on standards of assessment. The third topic is the effect of participation and self-appraisal, and the factors to be considered by any organization contemplating using self-appraisal. Some of the debates on assessment centres are examined next – their effectiveness, their costs relative to their merits and their impact on candidates. Finally, the role of the line manager in employee development is raised; this covers the question of whether managers understand their role and responsibilities in this area, and the problem of identifying the knowledge and skills possessed and needed for employee development. Where the evidence points in the direction of provisional conclusions on these issues, those conclusions are indicated, but the nature of these problems is such that one cannot generally offer all-embracing and definitive answers.

References

1. H.H. Meyer, E. Kay and J.P.R. French, Jr., 'Split roles in performance appraisal', *Harvard Business Review*, **43** (1965) pp. 123–9
   E. Kay, H.H. Meyer and J.R.P. French Jr., 'Effects of threat in a performance appraisal interview', *Journal of Applied Psychology*, **49** (1965) pp. 311–17
2 W.F. Nemeroff and K.N. Wexley, 'An exploration of the relationship between performance feedback interview characteristics and interview outcomes as perceived by managers and subordinates', *Journal of Occupational Psychology*, **52** (1979) pp. 25–34.
   R.J. Burke, W. Weitzel and T. Weir, 'Characteristics of effective employee performance review and development interviews: replication and extension', *Personnel Psychology*, **31** (1978), pp. 903–19.
3 M.M. Greller, 'The nature of subordinate participation in the appraisal interview', *Academy of Management Journal*, **21** (1978), pp. 646–54
4 L.L. Cummings, 'A field experimental study of the effects of two performance appraisal systems', *Personnel Psychology*, **26** (1973) pp. 489–502
   W.E. Beveridge, 'Attitudes to appraisal in three work organizations' *Management Education and Development*, **5** (1974) pp. 68–74.
   C.A. Fletcher, 'Interview style and the effectiveness of appraisal', *Occupational Psychology*, **47** (1973), pp. 225–30

C.A. Fletcher and R.S. Williams, 'The influence of performance feedback in appraisal interviews', *Journal of Occupational Psychology*, **49** (1976), pp. 75-83.

5   Kay *et al*, 'Effects of threat in a performance appraisal interview'.

6   Fletcher and Williams, 'The influence of performance feedback in appraisal interviews'.
     K.M. Brown, B.S. Willis and D.H. Reid, 'Differential effects of supervisor verbal feedback and feedback plus approval on institutional staff performance', *Journal of Organizational Behaviour Management*, **3** (1981), pp. 57–68

7   H.H. Meyer and W.B. Walker, 'A study of factors relating to the effectiveness of a performance appraisal program', *Personnel Psychology*, **14** (1961), pp. 291–8.

8   N.R.F. Maier, 'Three types of appraisal interview', *Personnel* (March/April 1958), pp. 27–40.

9   Fletcher and Williams, 'The influence of performance feedback in appraisal interviews'.

10   C.D. Fisher, 'Transmission of positive and negative feedback to subordinates: a laboratory investigation', *Journal of Applied Psychology*, **64** (1979) pp. 533–40.

11   C.A. Fletcher, 'Manager/subordinate communication and leadership style: a field study of their relationship to perceived outcomes of appraisal interviews', *Personnel Review*, **7** (1978) pp. 59–62.
     Greller, 'The nature of subordinate participation in the appraisal interview'.

12   ibid.

13   E.A. Locke and G.P. Latham, *Goal Setting: A Motivational Technique that Works* (Prentice-Hall 1984).

14   W.F. Nemeroff and J. Cosentino, 'Utilising feedback and goal setting to increase performance appraisal interviewer skills of managers', *Academy of Management Journal*, **22** (1979) pp. 566–76

15   K.H. Rowe, 'An appraisal of appraisals', *Journal of Management Studies*, **1** (1964), pp. 1–25.
     C.A. Fletcher, 'An evaluation study of job appraisal reviews', *Management Services in Government*, **28** (1973), pp. 188–95.

16   C.A. Fletcher, *An Appraisal of Appraisals: a Job Appraisal Review Evaluation Study in the Property Services Agency*, Behavioural Sciences Research Division Report No. 33 (Civil Service Department 1975).

17   R.S. Williams, J. Walker and C.A. Fletcher, 'International review of staff appraisal practices: current trends and issues,' *Public Personnel Management*, (January/February 1977) pp. 5–12.

18   J. Walker, C. Fletcher, R. Williams and K. Taylor, 'Performance appraisal: an open or shut case?' *Personnel Review*, **6** (1977), pp. 38–42.

19   A.R. Solem, 'Some supervisory problems in appraisal interviewing', *Personnel Administration*, **23** (1960), pp. 27–35.
     Fletcher, 'Interview style and the effectiveness of appraisal'.
     K.N. Wexley, J.P. Singh and G.A. Yukl, 'Subordinate personality as a moderator of the effects of participation in three types of appraisal interviews', *Journal of Applied Psychology*, **58** (1973) pp. 54–9
     J.M. Hillery and K.N. Wexley, 'Participation effects in appraisal interviews conducted in a training situation', *Journal of Applied Psychology*, **59** (1974) pp. 168–71
     M.M. Greller, 'Subordinate participation and reactions to the appraisal interview', *Journal of Applied Psychology*, **60** (1975) pp. 544–9.
     Nemeroff and Wexley, 'An exploration of the relationship between performance feedback interview characteristics and interview outcomes'.

20   B. Alban Metcalfe, 'Leadership behaviour in the appraisal interview – a critical summary of research findings and a proposal for a new methodology in future research', MRC/SSRC Social and Applied Psychology Unit paper (1982)

B. Alban Metcalfe, 'Effective appraisal interviewing', paper presented at the 7th NATO Leadership Symposium, Oxford (1982).

21 Greller, 'The nature of subordinate participation in the appraisal interview'.
Burke *et al*, 'Characteristics of effective employee performance review and development'.

22 Greller, 'The nature of subordinate participation in the appraisal interview'.

23 Fletcher, 'Manager/subordinate communication and leadership style'
E. Anstey, C. Fletcher and J. Walker, *Staff Appraisal and Development* (Allen and Unwin 1976).

24 P.J. Sadler and G.H. Hofstede, 'Leadership styles: preferences and perceptions of employees of an international company in different countries' *Mens En Onderneming*, **26** (1972), pp. 43–63.

25 H.H. Meyer 'Self appraisal of job performance,' *Personnel Psychology*, **33** (1980) pp. 291–5.

26 G.C. Thornton, 'Psychometric properties of self-appraisals of job performance', *Personnel Psychology*, **33** (1980), pp. 263–71.

27 H.H. Meyer, 'The use of self-assessments in performance appraisal', paper presented at the 20th International Congress of Applied Psychology, Edinburgh (1982).
G.A Bassett and H.H. Meyer, 'Performance appraisal based on self-review,' *Personnel Psychology*, **21**(1968), pp. 421–30.

28 S. Downs, R.M. Farr and L. Colbeck, 'Self-appraisal: a convergence of selection and guidance', *Journal of Occupational Psychology*, **51** (1978) pp. 271–8
G.P. Latham and K.N. Wexley, *Increasing Productivity Through Performance Appraisal* (Addison-Wesley, 1981).

29 H.G. Heneman, 'Self-assessment: a critical analysis', *Personnel Psychology*, **33** (1980), pp. 297–300.

30 R.S. Williams, 'Alternative raters and methods', in P. Herriot (ed.), *Assessment and Selection in Organizations* (Wiley 1989).

31 C.A. Fletcher, 'Self-assessment at work: introductory comments', paper presented to the 20th International Congress of Applied Psychology, Edinburgh (1982).

32 J. Heron 'Self and peer assessment', in T. Boydell and M. Pedler (eds.), *Management Self-Development* (Gower 1981).

33 J. Stinson and J. Stokes, 'How to multi-appraise', *Management Today* (June 1980), pp. 43, 45, 48, 53.

34 K.S. Teel, 'Self-appraisal revisited', *Personnel Journal*, **57** (1978), pp. 364–7.

35 Anstey et al, *Staff Appraisal and Development*.

36 B.B. Gaugler, D.B. Rosenthal, G.C. Thornton and C. Bentson, 'Meta-analysis of assessment center validity', *Journal of Applied Psychology*, **72** (1987), pp. 493–511.

37 E. Anstey, 'A 30 year follow-up of the CSSB procedure, with lessons for the future', *Journal of Occupational Psychology*, **50** (1977), pp. 149–59.

38 S.V. Dulewicz and C.A. Fletcher, 'The relationship between previous experience, intelligence and background characteristics of participants and their performance in an assessment centre', *Journal of Occupational Psychology*, **55** (1982), pp. 197–207.

39 I.T. Robertson and R.S. Kandola, 'Work sample tests: validity, adverse impact and applicant reaction', *Journal of Occupational Psychology*, **55** (1982), pp. 171–84.

40 B.Ungerson,'Assessment centres:a review of research findings', *Personnel Review*, **3** (1974), pp. 4–13.

41 C.A. Fletcher and S.V. Dulewicz, 'An empirical study of a UK-based assessment centre', *Journal of Management Studies*, **20** (1984).

42 E.E. Ghiselli, 'Intelligence and managerial success', *Psychological Reports*, **12** (1963), p. 898.

43 R. Gill, 'A trainability concept for management potential and an empirical study of its relationship with intelligence for two managerial skills', *Journal of Occupational Psychology*, **55** (1982), pp. 139–48.

44 A. Stewart and V. Stewart, *Tomorrow's Managers Today* (2nd edn) (Institute of Personnel Management 1981).

45 P.A. Iles and I.T. Robertson, 'The impact of personnel selection procedures on candidates', in P. Herriot (ed.), *Assessment and Selection in Organisations* (Wiley 1989).

46 S.V. Dulewicz and C.A. Fletcher, 'Does an assessment centre measure potential or experience? A comparison of US and UK findings on internal validity, attitudes and characteristics of participants', paper presented at the 10th International Congress on the Assessment Center Method, Pittsburgh, USA (1982).

47 C. Fletcher, 'Candidates' reactions to assessment centres and their outcomes: a longitudinal study', *Journal of Occupational Psychology* (1991), pp. 117–27.

48 J.W. Walker, 'Does career planning rock the boat?', *Human Resource Management* (1978), pp. 2–7.

8
Future challenges and opportunities

In Chapter 1 we touched on the broader social and economic changes of the day which provide a backdrop for contemporary personnel practice, and at various points we have described performance appraisal and career development (PA/CD) systems which, to some extent, reflect these broader social changes. Today's social, economic, and technological developments bring with them major employment policy issues which, some contend,[1] will remain with us for the rest of the century. If this is true, then many of the challenges and opportunities of the future are with us already. And it is our view that PA/CD systems have not come very far in meeting these challenges and opportunities. The purpose of this chapter, therefore, is to pick up the historical theme begun in Chapter 1, by considering today's, and tomorrow's, employment policy issues and the implications and questions they raise for PA and CD.

Careers: changing attitudes and patterns

While it remains true that the individual's career continues to occupy an important place in life as a whole, it increasingly is the case that people are striving for a better balance between work and non-work. Guerrier and Philpot,[2] surveying a group of British managers, found for example that:

> 'Whilst managers are concerned about their careers, they are equally concerned about their home and family life. Numerous comments on the difficulties of finding time for family and leisure activities whilst coping with a demanding job indicate the potential for conflict between these two areas of their life.'

As many writers[3] have pointed out, work and family lives mutually interact, but this is not to say that everyone displays the same pattern of interrelationships. For instance, Evans and Bartolomé[4] discuss five patterns, concluding that a spillover relationship is the most common. They reported that for the managers and wives they studied this spillover relationship was very largely one way:

> 'Professional life affects the quality of private life on a day-to-day basis. But the reverse is not true; private life only affects the quality of professional life in extreme situations. The effect of private life on professional life is through its influence on major career and life decisions.'

And, for people seeking to enter employment, non-work considerations impinge on the decision. Thus, Kitwood,[5] in a study of adolescents, identifies a group for whom there is an issue of 'whether or not to try to form a career', and all that goes with this question:

> 'There is the matter of whether the social life of school is tolerable; whether there is sufficient money for current needs; the plans of friends; obligations to the family; the availability-of jobs in the locality.'

Today, these issues have become even more acute for young people, and a recent development in secondary education is the teaching of 'life skills'. In work-related terms these skills include finding and keeping a job, changing jobs, and balancing work with the rest of life. Such skills are needed as much by adults in employment, as by adolescents making the transition from school. Life/career planning workshops are offered by a few organizations, but there is here a considerable unmet need. And it is one which organizations may feel reluctant to meet. After all, decisions about work and family, for example, are very much matters for the individuals concerned. Yet these decisions may have implications for the organization. There is therefore a balance to be struck between the organization being over-intrusive in personal decision-making (and perhaps appearing to be paternalistic) or showing little or no interest whatsoever. Between these two extremes, there is scope for the organization to help people with their decision-making, to the mutual benefit of both parties. Much of this book is about ways in which people can be more involved in decisions about their careers.

Changing conceptions of careers
One of the advantages that will result from life-skills teaching in schools is that young people will be more aware of the need for a changed view of careers and career development. It is probably fair to say that academic analyses of the concept of career are somewhat ahead of much contemporary organizational practice, and are out of step with individuals' views. Although more and more people are coming to review the place of their career in their lives as a whole, it remains the case that the 'upward and onward' view remains the most prevalent conception of what a career is all about. There is no doubt that the climate of the day calls for individuals to modify their thinking about careers; there needs to be a shift away from the advancement orientation. Organizations, too, need to change their career

development practices so that more emphasis is given to lateral movement and we shall return to this later in the chapter.

Equal employment opportunity considerations

Women

It is worth noting that the earlier comments about careers and families related to studies of men. Is the position for women different? It is difficult to answer this question with any certainty because women in employment are now only beginning to receive serious study. But there is evidence of an apparent desire on the part of women to return to work after a period of bringing up children. The increase in the labour force by over two million between 1961 and 1980 can be accounted for by this.

Although more women are economically active now than twenty years ago, in other respects the position of women in employment has not changed. Even though the proportion of women entering employment has risen, it still is the case that women are under-represented here, particularly at the uppermost levels. Women are under-represented in the professions, and they are few and far between in the higher reaches of the trade union movement. By contrast, women are in the majority in low-grade white- and blue-collar employment. And the evidence[6] suggests that patterns of occupational segregation have not changed greatly over several decades. One might have expected the Sex Discrimination Act (SDA) to have had a significant impact on occupational segregation, but it has, in practice, been slight. And the impact of the SDA on women's employment in other respects has been slight too: few employers take advantage of the positive provisions, and few women make use of the opportunities the Act affords them.

The disappointing impact of the SDA leads to the conclusion that the law itself is only a partial solution to the problem of discrimination. For some organizations and individuals it would appear that the law is a sufficient reason to change. Some have done so voluntarily, while others have done so because they have in some way experienced the provisions of the law. Thus, case law has built up and this now provides a valuable guide for employers. Some of the cases which have been heard have been assisted and financed by the Equal Opportunities Commission (EOC), and this is one of the ways in which the EOC will continue to press for change; the EOC's power to conduct formal investigations is another example. Thus, the EOC remains a source of pressure. And there are several others. The rate of decline of men's employment is expected to be more rapid than that of women; the proportion of women (and their absolute numbers), therefore, will remain high. A great many women's groups exist – for example, Women in the Civil Service, The

Women's Engineering Society, Women in Banking, and Women in Computing. Some activity is being seen on the part of the trade unions to promote equality of opportunity, and there will also be the influence of EC directives. Multinationals of North American parentage operating in the UK will also be a force for positive action. Professional groups, such as the Institute of Personnel Management, will continue to press for change.

Notwithstanding all these pressures, an organization can still decline to act. But the failure to do anything could perhaps be seen as condoning unlawful behaviour on the part of the managers. It also means that more will have to be done later. To do nothing and hope that difficulties will go away is an unhealthy strategy; eventually the point will be reached when the difficulties become so great that change is preferable. But this *reactive* stance places the organization in the position of having to retrieve a situation which in some manner has gone wrong. It is far better to have a positive and proactive management strategy. This demonstrates the company's social responsibility. It allows the organization to be ready with a defence should it be faced with an allegation of unlawful discrimination. The promotion of equality of opportunity enhances a company's image – fighting a discrimination case is likely to lead to a bad press, as well as being costly. Organizations need to develop their best talent irrespective of the sex or race of individuals. Policies and practices which discriminate on these grounds are inherently ineffective. Equal employment opportunity is thus good business sense, and is being recognized as such by various organizations. One illustration of this is the National Westminister Bank's re-entry and retainer scheme described in Example 8.1.

This illustration also shows a way in which some of the impediments to women's career development can be overcome. There are various reasons why the position of women in employment has not changed greatly. Partly it is because of *systemic barriers in organizations' policies*, partly because of the *attitudes of management*, and partly because of the *attitudes of women* themselves. And from each of these three sets of reasons various practical implications flow.

For organizations, a major implication is that they should review their policies and procedures. Are women included in appraisal schemes? If so, do they fare as well as men? That is, are the distributions of performance and potential ratings comparable for the two groups?) Are women eligible for management development programmes equally with men? Large numbers of women are in part-time employment, and part-timers are often treated as some kind of 'second class' employee. There should be an appraisal scheme for them, whether women or men. They should also be eligible for career development opportunities – whether alongside full-timers or through a

---

Example 8.1 *The National Westminster Bank's re-entry and retainer scheme for career orientated women*[7]

The scheme is intended primarily for women who have left the bank to have a family and who wish to return after a break of a number of years. The scheme is seen as a contribution to the Bank's search for women managers of the future. Therefore the women selected for it must have demonstrated career potential and commitment during their early years with the Bank. The scheme has a number of operating principles, including the following:

- The women can maintain contact with the Bank for a maximum period of five years.

- They must undertake at least two weeks of relief work a year, for which they are paid.

- The Bank agrees to consider them during the five years for vacancies at the previous level or grade of appointment and to provide whatever training is needed on their return.

- Any woman who is guaranteed re-entry should continue to study for the Institute of Banking examinations if they have not already been completed.

The scheme is in its early days, but it is seen as making good business sense. It allows the Bank to tap a considerable reservoir of talent and experience which might otherwise have been under-utilized or lost altogether.

Expected benefits include the following:

- A team of relief staff to act as a cushion to cover known periods of pressure ...

- A register of potential applicants of known ability and experience ...

- A means of attracting and retaining female recruits of high potential.

- 'Role models' which will, it is hoped, persuade line managers that it is possible to combine family and career. At the same time, and as more women are seen climbing higher up the career ladder, they may change other women's perception of the part they can play in the organization.

- The re-entry package is a practical demonstration of the Bank's commitment to genuine equality of opportunity.

---

separate scheme is for the organization to decide. Organizations should make greater use of the law's positive action provisions.

Reviewing policies and procedures is a step on the way towards overcoming managerial resistance and lack of understanding, but other actions are also needed. Training courses should deal with equal employment opportunity issues. For example, the design of appraisal training should enable course members to explore their perceptions of the performance of women at work. Training in promotion interviewing, counselling, and other kinds of management training lend themselves to treatment in a similar fashion. The organization may also choose to offer courses focusing specifically on men and women at work.

As regards the women themselves, various questions might be asked. If their performance truly is less good than that of men, can the apparent deficiency be corrected in some way? Perhaps a change of job is required, or a training course – according to the particular need, this may or may not be single sex training as allowed by the positive action provisions of the Sex Discrimination Act. Do women fail to apply for development opportunities? If so, why? It may be that they do not know that the opportunities exist. Or it may be because of lack of confidence on their part. Similarly this is a reason which may apply to women who do not take up development opportunities offered to them. Women-only training (as illustrated in Example 6.1) may be an appropriate response to this, but such training needs to be reinforced by the other kinds of actions described otherwise there is a risk of the effects being dissipated.

Dual-career couples

The large number of women in employment has introduced another career management issue – that of the dual-career couple. It is often asserted that women, married or otherwise, work just for the money, or for social reasons. This may be true for some women (and men, for that matter) in two-worker families, but such reasons do not apply to all women; it is likely that, on the whole, women work for much the same reasons as men. Therefore, more and more women may be expected to demonstrate a career commitment equal to that shown by men; hence the dual-career couple. This phenomenon may well lead to an increasingly stressful life style for the partners in such couples; family decisions become more difficult as do decisions about careers. These difficult choices can be aggravated by organizational policies and practices.

What, more specifically, will the phenomenon of the dual-career couple mean for individuals and organizations? Whereas in the traditional family it was the man's career decisions which made the impact, now and in the future there will be cases where either or both spouses may be faced with important career decisions which have family implications.

For partners in such couples there may be an increased reluctance to make job transfers (at the same level or on promotion) if they involve a geographical move, which could prove to be disrupting to the other partner's career. The reluctance to move may be heightened still further if children's education is also to be considered.

In this way, therefore, dual careers exacerbate an organizational problem which already exists. How tolerant or flexible is the organization prepared to be in the application of its policies? The employee may turn down career moves. How many refusals will the organization allow before concluding that the individual isn't interested in further career development? Sensitivity is needed here and in the broader application of mobility policies; and to be sensitive to these issues means that the organization has to do something, for example the provision of career counselling so that family and domestic considerations can be taken into account (by employee and organization alike). Organizations are able to offer inducements to encourage geographical career moves, but where the employee is part of a dual-career family the organization may need to direct inducements towards the spouse also. This may mean finding a suitable career opportunity for the spouse who might otherwise be adversely affected by the move.

An organizational response such as this therefore increases the likelihood of the employee accepting the transfer. Where one partner does move, the couple may decide that their interests are best served by adapting their life styles for a period. For example, one option is for the couple to decide to live between two homes. Another option is for one partner to commute long distances. Where there are two incomes, a wider range of responses of these kinds may be feasible, especially if they are assisted (financially) by the organization (as they can be).

Minority groups
Much of what has been said about women applies equally to members of racial or ethnic groups. For example, their representation in management, the professions, and the like is disproportionately low. Also, they are under-represented in skilled occupations at lower levels. As with women, systemic barriers serve to work against minorities, as do prejudicial attitudes on the part of many employers and co-workers.

The sorts of actions discussed already are therefore appropriate, and some progress is being made. There have been significant developments in the past few years involving, for example, police cadet recruitment, language training for minorities, recruitment training at the Ford Motor Company; and many local authorities have appointed officers with special responsibilities for minorities (and for women, too). But there remain many gaps. For instance, performance appraisal training on the whole does little to help managers explore their attitudes towards minorities at work. (And this is probably true of many other kinds of management training.) At best one tends only to see bland statements of the kind 'thou shalt not discriminate', whereas there is a need for much more specific 'do's and don'ts' and training to increase managers' understanding and awareness of minorities. The use of the repertory grid technique or carefully scripted film or closed circuit TV vignettes or narrative case studies have a part to play here.

Though not strictly an equal opportunity issue, it is appropriate at this point to draw a comparison between the career management of minority groups and similar problems experienced by multinational organizations with, for example, the career management of employees of national origins other than that of the parent organization, or the transfer of, say, British management culture to a local workforce overseas. Whilst one might hope for some similarities across cultures, the likelihood is that cultural differences – for example, legislative procedures, social customs, beliefs about work – will severely limit the application of career management policy developed in one country to another. Evidence pertinent to these differences comes from various sources. One source, for example, is a survey[8] of performance appraisal practices in a number of public administrations around the world. This shows the impact of legislative provisions. In the US there are Equal Employment Opportunities laws, and various administrative regulations, providing a stringent framework within which a foreign company operating in the US would have to operate. In Germany, there is legislation which gives employees the right of access to their personal files; in the US the Freedom of Information Act operates in a similar way. Thus, in some countries openness is, in effect, mandated, and it is not an issue in the way that it is in this country. Quite apart from any formal legislative provision, a nation's value systems need to be considered. To take Germany again as an example, openness there is 'considered a positive social achievement' affording protection 'against prejudices of . . . superiors that cannot be supported by facts'. Other evidence comes from Bass and his colleagues[9] who have carried out studies on the assessment of managers in different countries. They conclude that '. . . career success in management is associated with various personal attributes which may differ in different locations'. And they highlight the difficulties of interpersonal communication as a stumbling block to the transfer of personnel technology and introducing change; it is in the '. . . area of person-to-person relationships that the greatest opportunities for conflict, misunderstanding and resistance to change are most likely when people from different countries and cultures must work together'. So, as with the management of ethnic minorities in this country, there is a great need to understand the values and culture of the foreign nationals, whether they be in their own country working under British management transferred overseas, or whether they be working in Britain on some kind of temporary assignment.

However, necessary though such understanding is, it is far from being the only consideration. Where foreign nationals are involved there is a need to be flexible in adapting existing systems; indeed flexibility seems to be a key word when it comes to the application of PA and CD systems. And, as with any PA system, there is a need for those who will use the system to be appropriately trained. Yet another consideration centres on the adoption of a standard approach to performance appraisal in the various countries where the multinational operates. The use of a standard approach certainly has advantages for career development purposes – facilitating cross-national transfers and comparisons – yet it runs the risk of overlooking important cultural variations and suchlike. So, our general principle about developing PA and CD systems in an empirical fashion holds true.

As to the career management of British nationals sent overseas, there are particular implications for selection and training. It is evident that skills in dealing with people are highly important. Technical competence, too, will be required. In both of these areas the nature and level of skill needed will be a consequence of the nature and level of job to be performed. This, in other words, is a straightforward selection problem. But, as may happen with home-based selection decisions, it is often the case that the selection is too heavily influenced by technical competence at the expense of relational ability. Beyond this, there are problems of adjustment (to the new environment and culture) to be faced, not only by the expatriates themselves but also by their families. Training of some kind may be an appropriate response, exactly what training being dependent upon the adjustment required.[10]

Do people want to participate in decisions about their career?

Surveying a group of British managers, Guerrier and Philpott[11] found that their particular sample wanted influence over the way things are run at work. And in reviews[12] of the evidence on participation it is suggested that people want immediate participation with their supervisors on job-related issues and that an increase in participation can enhance individual well-being at work. By inference, therefore, one might surmise from this evidence about direct participation that people do want to have more of a say in decisions about their careers.

Such a sweeping generalization is unlikely to hold true for everyone of course: a range of views about individual participation in career planning is to be expected. Routledge and Elliot[13] discuss studies bearing on this and identify two characteristic patterns of career development.

One pattern seems to imply a certain degree of passivity on the part of the individual: '. . . a more accommodating approach to career development, and a belief that development is subservient to the needs of the organisation.' The other type of pattern shows much more proactivity: an '... aggressiveness towards career development and a belief that a career is the individual's responsibility and is determined by his actions.'

It is noteworthy that much of the recent literature about careers, and other publications such as Handy,[14] encourage people to adopt this latter stance, and our earlier comments about career and family suggest that such proactivity is becoming much more evident. Indeed, for individuals who are interested in career development it may be that more assertiveness on their part is needed if they are to secure the available promotions. But where does this leave the rather passive individuals? They are the ones most likely to stay put in the organization. Some may be perfectly content as they are. Others, perhaps, are lacking in confidence and, as a consequence, do not put themselves forward. (This view is often held about women, for example.) In any event, some responsibility rests with the employing organization to set an appropriately encouraging climate through the use of career counselling and workshops. Passive about their careers though they may be, these employees nonetheless represent an important organizational resource. To do nothing about their career development will ultimately be dysfunctional. Organizational passivity only reinforces individual passivity, with obsolescence, lack of morale and motivation, and perhaps resentment being the eventual consequences.

Slower growth and high expectations: a major conflict

Manpower planning

What we see in today's generally recessionary climate are various conflicting pressures. On the one hand, the economic situation is leading to organizational contraction. People at all levels are being laid off. There are fewer and fewer advancement opportunities. There is low demand for new staff. And the impact of new technology may make this worse in some sectors of employment, although others may experience a degree of growth. On the other hand, employee expectations have risen, fostered by the period of growth up to the mid-1970s. Expectations have moderated somewhat in the past few years, and, with the economic climate as it is, simply having a job counts for much for many people. But for others aspirations are still high and discontent about career progress may manifest itself through turnover or wastage. But not all discontented employees will leave.

What is to be done about them? And what should be done for the satisfied stayers? The two sets of conflicting pressures described here –

that is, organizational and employee needs – are the core elements of manpower planning, or human resource planning[15] (to use a term more popular today). And the essential requirement is for these to be maintained in state of balance.

As this is not a book about manpower planning *per se*, it is sufficient for present purposes to point out the need for an overall framework which manpower planning can provide and into which PA and CD practices must fit. And, because of this, manpower planning is not, in our view, solely, or even primarily, about forecasting numbers. Contemporary views about manpower planning are much broader in scope and reflect the increasing concern to derive human resource plans from overall organization plans. But, more than this, human resource plans, and their multifarious behavioural consequences (for example, promotions, transfers, levels of morale) must feed back into organizational plans – in other words, the actions of people have consequences for organizational planning. This is often overlooked. An emphasis on behavioural implications is to be found in the work of the Institute for Manpower Studies, and the interested reader is referred to their publications[16] for more information. Of more immediate concern here is to return to the conflicting pressures described in the previous paragraph, and to elaborate on them further. First for consideration is organizational contraction and its implications.

Unemployment

In recent years a lot of research has been carried out on people who have become unemployed. One recent study, by Swinburne,[17] looked at male managers and professionals. She reported that they felt shock and fear and uncertainty about the future, and there were some feelings of loss of self-respect. Of particular interest is the finding that 'the degree of warning or control which was given in relation to unemployment was an important factor in the intensity of negative feelings experienced, which in turn tended to affect the ease with which unemployment was handled.' Thus, one obvious implication for employers is to give as much warning as possible of redundancy, so that it does not come like a bolt out of the blue. And giving plenty of notice may help the employee come to feel that he or she has some degree of control or influence over the sequence of events – both psychological and material.

Managing redundancy

The decision to declare redundancies – whether voluntary or compulsory – may be the inevitable last resort for the organization. Where this is so, there is much that can be done to manage the redundancy programme so that stress is reduced.

As well as giving as much warning as possible (which of course is dependent on the immediacy of the redundancy problem), the organization can provide more tangible help and support. Financial advice is likely to be particularly valuable. So, too, is a personal counselling service, or perhaps career/life planning workshops, not only to help people cope with the redundancy itself but also so that they can reappraise their positions – in other words, another illustration of self-appraisal. As Hayes[18] has pointed out, many of the helping efforts directed at unemployed people seem to assume that unemployment is a temporary phenomenon. For some, this may be true, and help in acquiring job-finding or presentational skills, or help in setting up their own businesses may be of value. In this way, redundancy will mean a radical career change. But for others, long-term unemployment may be the prospect and adjusting to this can be a painful process. Exactly what sort of help the organization needs to provide will be governed partly by the magnitude of the redundancies, but it need not be assumed that a large number of lay-offs presents an insurmountable challenge: Example 8.2, describing the British Steel Corporation's demonstration of organizational and social responsibility in action, is a case in point.

An underlying question remains, though – 'How do we decide who we are to make redundant?' On the basis of seniority? Closing down a plant and moving production elsewhere? Age? Asking for volunteers? By going for the last option the organization relinquishes some control over who goes and runs the risk of losing some talented people or having too many takers. If the latter happens then the organization is still faced with having to decide whom to lay off. And the organization again has the problem of having to choose. Is performance a criterion, perhaps? According to a recent IPM survey,[20] organizations claimed that work performance was a major criterion in selecting senior executives for redundancy, yet the researchers were able to find, in practice, only a few examples of rigorous procedures to identify low performers to be earmarked for redundancy. So, is there yet another purpose here to be added to those of the PA system? And is the system up to it? Or would the knowledge that PA might be used to get rid of people through redundancy simply induce line managers to give generous narratives and inflated ratings? This, in other words, is comparable to the promotion pressure: the fact that there are fewer opportunities may lead appraisers to boost their assessment so as to give their people a chance of being considered for promotion, or to reduce the likelihood of them being laid off.

Career discontent

External mobility
We argued earlier that, despite the prevailing recessionary climate, the aspirations of many employees remain high. Faced with limited

---

Example 8.2   *Counselling for redundant staff –
the British Steel Corporation programme*[19]

The massive reduction in the BSC workforce – a planned 50 per cent cut
over a ten-year period – led the Corporation to provide a personal
counselling service, available to anyone being made redundant who
wished to avail themselves of it.

The counsellors are either volunteers or nominated by management or
by the union. An intensive seven-day training programme is provided for
the prospective counsellors and this acts as a vehicle for self-selection;
advice and feedback from the counselling and tutorial staff are provided to
feed the self-selection process.

The counselling team is representative of the age, service and
occupational composition of the workforce, and individual counsellors are
knowledgeable about the working environment, the job content and skills
of the workforce they counsel, and about the community and social life of
the area. The employment position of the employee-turned-counsellor does
not change; he or she may be as much at risk as any of the other members
of staff.

Use of the counselling service is entirely voluntary, but those who do
not come forward are nonetheless offered an appointment; there is, of
course, no obligation to attend. The take-up rate has been high, personal
interviews having been given to about 100,000 employees. It has been
found that the opportunity to discuss problems and receive advice has
been welcomed. Counselling has provided an effective means of
communication; it has provided an opportunity to correct ill-founded
rumours, it has helped people accept the inevitable change and to prepare
for it; it has encouraged people to review their options; and it has helped
people acquire personal development and self-management skills.

---

advancement opportunities within their own organization, many of the
most marketable employees will vote with their feet and leave – this
despite the fact that jobs can be hard to find. Sometimes called wastage
or turnover, external mobility is a common enough phenomenon and is
particularly high amongst relatively new entrants to an organization.
For example, during the first few years at work approximately 50 per
cent of early school leavers change jobs at least once.[21] For graduates,
one recent survey[22] has shown similar levels of turnover over a five- or
six-year time span. Of particular interest in this survey of graduates
are their reasons for leaving: many '... felt their abilities were not
being used, were dissatisfied with the general nature and pace of work,
and saw limited opportunities for career development ahead of them'.

Admittedly, these are the views of leavers only; we do not know what
the stayers felt. But even so, the implications of such reactions cannot

be disregarded. They may well be an indicator of the extent to which occupational aspirations and expectations rose during the late 1970s, coupled with the fact that there now are more young people with more years of education and more qualifications. There are, therefore, considerable risks for organizations, such as the risk of taking on staff who are too well qualified for the job. Graduate clerks are not uncommon, and, quite apart from this, it is already the case that many young new entrants are brighter and more able (albeit less experienced) than their bosses. This phenomenon is likely to become increasingly apparent. How are the parties involved going to cope? Some supervisors may simply seek to hold on to their good people. Other bosses may fear that they will be displaced by their younger subordinates. And these reactions may be reflected in the appraisal report. Also, the appraisal discussion may become harder to carry out, an experience that cuts both ways affecting appraiser and appraisee alike. Consider, for example, the research finding that managers who are substantially more intelligent than their subordinates tend to be less effective as leaders than where the intelligence differential is less marked. Similarly, where a wide gap is created by the subordinate being more intelligent, this too may work against effective leadership. It may end up with two parties talking near different languages in the appraisal interview, and all sorts of negative reactions may develop. The manager may feel he has to struggle to keep in control of the interview, and he may even feel some resentment. The subordinate may feel that his ability isn't being recognized or fully utilized; he may not get the feedback that he needs on his performance; and he may feel that the manager does not understand his point of view.

Such difficulties as these reinforce the need for effective training in performance management – managers letting their staff know what is expected of them, giving regular feedback, appraisal interviewing skills, and so on. Other management actions to reduce these risks include well-designed induction programmes, which include training for managers and careful matching of new entrants and initial supervisors (where this is possible).[23] Action can also be taken at the recruitment stage by not recruiting people who are too well qualified for the jobs on offer, and by providing more realistic information about those jobs so as to help applicants self-select themselves out of the running.[24]

External mobility takes place at higher levels too, and some increase in managerial mobility appears to have taken place over the past couple of decades.[25] Such external mobility, at whatever level and however caused (voluntary or otherwise), can, depending upon the circumstances, be looked upon as a good thing. It provides opportunities for internal mobility, allows the introduction of 'new blood', or (from a more cynical point of view) permits the shedding of staff at relatively low cost. But there are risks as well: the rate of turnover may be too high, talented staff may leave, or remaining staff may become discontented.

Internal mobility

Exactly how much external mobility an organization needs, or can tolerate, is an issue to be faced in manpower planning; and it is another issue of balance. The balance required is that between the demands for external mobility and those for internal mobility – for example, promotions, lateral transfers.

During contraction, internal mobility is extremely difficult to bring about, of course, but the need for it is great, and it does have certain benefits. With fewer promotion opportunities, mobility at the same level provides for continued career development – particularly for the 'plateaued' employee, for instance. And it does offer some scope for employees disappointed with their career progress. It promotes flexibility and versatility and broadens experience, thereby reducing the risk of obsolescence or 'burn out' amongst employees. Also, it can encourage commitment to the organization by showing that there are still opportunities and that the organization continues to value its employees. This last benefit can, however, sometimes turn into a disadvantage, especially if it is true, as some[26] have asserted, that '... the ability of an employer to offer life-long employment is becoming less and less the norm ...'. How true this statement is for any one organization depends, naturally enough, upon its particular organizational and manpower plans and how they are operated.

Some organizations have a tradition of encouraging internal mobility; job rotation, for instance, has long been recognized as a developmental activity, but has often been confined to the flyers. It needs to be applied much more widely.

Organizations will need to question the adequacy of their existing procedures for facilitating lateral transfers. Does the appraisal system yield relevant information to help the organization decide where to move people? Who will take the decisions about lateral moves? Personnel managers? Line managers? Panels comprising both? The successful use of panels or committees to manage personnel planning is illustrated in Example 8.3. Other questions about lateral moves are to do with the involvement of the individual. Does the organization provide career information to help people make their own choices about available opportunities? Leaflets or booklets, films or videotapes, lectures or discussions conducted by senior staff, are all means which can be used to convey career information to staff. Advertising the vacancies is another issue, and many well-established procedures exist; for example, posting vacancies on noticeboards and the use of company newspapers or job vacancy bulletins are popular methods. Activities such as these are needed not only because they have participative

Example 8.3   *Personnel planning committees –*
balancing organizational and individual needs[27]

This North American company, in the telecommunications industry, has
about 13,000 employees. About 4000 are managers/professionals, some
1200 of these having supervisory responsibilities.

The company has a formalised network of personnel planning
committees. Committees at any one managerial level are responsible for
the identification, development, and movement of managerial staff at the
next lower level. The committees at the upper levels of management
operate company-wide; at middle levels they are organized by function;
and below this the committees represent the company's various staff and
field areas. Line managers serve on the committees with personnel acting
in a service capacity.

The committees work to an annual planning cycle. This begins with the
preparation of biographical and career development profiles on each
manager (written by the supervisor). Running concurrently with this
exercise is the completion of annual performance assessments. These two
sets of information are drawn upon by the planning committees as a basis
for the annual assessment of potential. This assessment can be updated
half-yearly if required.

As well as assessing potential, the committees develop managers'
career plans and throughout the year they meet to fill managerial
vacancies and make management transfers. Movement of managers
between functions increased from 5 per cent to 50 per cent over a ten-year
period, a development which the company sees as a major strength of the
planning committees.

Participation by individual managers in their career planning is
encouraged through an annual survey of career interests. This allows
managers to express preferences either for specific jobs or types of work.
Managers can also express interest in job vacancies as they occur during
the year. Comprehensive information about jobs is made available by
means of a directory of all jobs in the company. A career planning guide is
issued along with the other survey materials.

value, but also because they have an important place in the
management of career disappointment. In this respect, the main
outcomes of counselling and workshops will be more realistic
expectations on the part of employees, the acceptance of a changing
view of career development, and an understanding of their
responsibilities for their careers. True, there is some risk – that of
having talented people leave – but this is an ever-present risk, and we
know of no reason to believe that participative approaches to career
management and planning add to that risk.

Increasing numbers of organizations have come to discover that their internal labour markets now have to be managed in a more purposeful way than in the past. No longer is it possible to rely on the traditional methods – wastage and promotions – to create development opportunities. Other methods have to be sought to maintain the vitality of the career development system, and the vitality of employees. What an organization can do depends on a number of factors, size being particularly important. A large group clearly has more scope for managing mobility. For smaller organizations, there may be scope for enriching jobs so that they provide a more challenging experience.[28] Temporary secondments, or interchanges, with other organizations might be set up. Doing so can be time-consuming, but, provided the secondment is a real job, there are significant benefits to be gained.[29] These include broadening of experience, acquiring new knowledge and skills, and personal development such as increased confidence or revitalization. Sabbaticals, too, merit consideration. But these kinds of 'temporary' external mobility need careful management if they are to succeed; in particular, the eventual re-entry of the employee needs to be planned well in advance.

Promotions

So far we have referred to two broad categories of employees. First, there are those whom the organization wishes to lose for one reason or another. Second, there are those whom the organization sees as good performers and wishes to retain, but who are seen as having no further advancement potential in today's limiting climate. These comprise the biggest group of employees within organizations. Then there is a third category: the people the organization wishes to promote.

Already there are fewer promotions available than in the past, and in most sectors of employment the position is unlikely to improve. Organizations, therefore, will have to be much more rigorous in their internal selection procedures. Will there be a place for PA in these? For some organizations the answer will be a clear 'No': PA will be highly orientated towards employee development. For others, the role of PA may be much reduced, appraisal reports being one (hopefully small) part of a promotion system incorporating other assessment devices. Still others will respond to the pressures for greater accuracy by developing their appraisal system in a professionally thorough and rigorous fashion, although, as we saw in the previous chapter, the prospects for an especially high degree of accuracy, are not encouraging. At the same time, these organizations will attempt to respond to employee needs through techniques such as self-appraisal, or by experimenting with some form of multiple appraisal, of which Example 8.4 represents an illustration. Multiple appraisal is extremely rare, yet there are many working situations in which parties other than the employee and the immediate supervisor can make a meaningful contribution

Example 8.4   *An experiment in multiple appraisal*[30]

This experimental programme, developed by the Gulf Oil Corporation, was introduced to help combat what were seen as three main problems with the company's existing performance appraisal system. First, the system was seen as relying too heavily on the immediate line manager. Second, the assessment of performance was not made against job-related criteria. Third, insufficient emphasis was given to performance improvement.

The experimental programme was designed to supplement, rather than supplant, the normal system, as it was felt that formal evaluation was a necessary prerequisite to recommending wider application. The main features of the experimental system were that it incorporated the views of others who were part of the work network of the person being assessed, and it provided for self-assessment; and the assessment criteria were represented by a multiple-role definition of the managerial job. A total of thirty senior executives, based in eight countries throughout Europe, took part in the programme. There were five steps in the programme, as follows:

1   The participants each self-selected between five and eight raters whom they believed to be in a position to make a useful assessment of their performance. Self-selection of the raters was regarded as important as it increases the acceptance of feedback. The participant sent each rater a Rating Form (described below) with a covering letter requesting completion of the form and its return, anonymously, to the Human Resources Department. At the same time the rater was told how the participant would receive feedback.

2   The completed Rating Forms were analysed by the Human Resources Department to produce a Summary Feedback Form for each participant.

3   A copy of the Summary Feedback Form was sent to each participant and their immediate bosses (who had been briefed previously on what was to happen). Either party could go to the Human Resources Department for clarification of any of the information on the form.

4   Each participant was asked to complete a self-appraisal, having regard to the content of the Summary Feedback Form. The form used for this purpose was the usual Corporate Performance Appraisal Form. This was then sent on to the immediate boss.

5   Based on the Summary Feedback Form, the self-appraisal and their own views, the bosses next completed a Corporate Performance Appraisal Form and then held an interview with the participant.

The Rating Form for the experiment had three main elements: an overall assessment of job performance; an analysis of managerial effectiveness against a seven-factor model of managerial behaviour; and a narrative assessment citing specific incidents to elaborate on the seven-factor analysis. The model of managerial behaviour was largely developed intuitively, although it drew on relevant published research and the outcome of an internal job evaluation exercise. In completing this part of the form the raters had to select the two roles which they felt the participant performed the most effectively, and the two performed least effectively, so as to identify areas in which improvement was needed.

The evaluation showed a high degree of acceptance, by both participants and bosses, of the job improvement information, although it is recognized that the approach can be threatening for some. Interestingly, the information communicated was found to be highly specific. Furthermore, there was no evidence that over-rating had taken place as a result of multiple appraisal. It is believed that the anonymity built into the procedure was essential in encouraging greater honesty.

to the appraisal. An organization may choose to tap these other sources of information in an informal way, but this may lead to abuse and even greater inaccuracy. Therefore, a structured means of obtaining and integrating the information is required if it is to be acceptable and useful. With the marked drop in promotions which has taken place (and which will stay with us), the use of PA as a major element in promotion procedures seems to be hard to defend. After all, promotion opportunities are going to be available for only a small percentage of employees. Furthermore, there is the argument that the use of PA results for decision-making purposes of this kind acts as a pressure leading to reduced discriminability amongst assessments (and hence people), or inflated assessments, or both. If this line of argument is correct then it is clear that the use of PA in this way is self-defeating! Such a PA system, therefore, yields information that is less than useful for promotion purposes, thereby putting more pressure on other elements of the decision-making procedure. And the information is less than useful for developmental purposes, too, if the appraisers have been led to write bland appraisal reports. Whichever course is taken, the end result is likely to be much the same: there will be greater reliance on other approaches to assessing potential, most probably assessment centres so as to exploit the developmental side-benefits as well.

New technology

While it is true that there is a broad role for the personnel and training functions in the management of new technology projects, our concern here is with how microelectronic technology can help these functions in the management of career development. We look at three areas of application – computerized personnel information systems, computers in career planning, and the provision of career information by computer.

Computerized personnel information system

Such systems, and computer-based training, are hardly new ideas, but it is the increased availability of mini- and microcomputers which has rendered these applications more feasible than they have hitherto been. Fuller treatment of these topics may be found elsewhere;[31] for the present it is sufficient to concentrate more narrowly on selected issues to do with purposes and information needs.

Decisions about purposes are crucial because they determine what kind of information needs to be recorded and how the system is to be used (and technical considerations such as size and type of system). Typically, the information recorded about people is biographical and career-related – for example, date of birth, date of joining, details of present post, qualifications, and the like. Whether the system should hold historical data – previous jobs, training received – will be a matter for the organization to decide. Similarly, should the system record performance appraisal data? This is a contentious matter, the purpose of the system being one of the considerations to be taking into account. If one of the purposes is to assist in career planning and development, then these kinds of information will be needed. But then there are other questions to do with security, confidentiality and access to information. At the moment, in some organizations, performance ratings are confidential, that is, they are not seen by the individual. Transferring these data to a computer record may put the organization in the position of having to make the ratings available to individuals if they wish to know what information the computer holds about them.

Thus, computerization may force the issue of openness. But this is only one issue of many, which range from such practical considerations as how you get the data on the computer – for example, shall we see machine-scoreable appraisal forms? – to the much broader question of how the system will be used. For instance, it is possible that computerization will enable you to do additional things not presently achievable (or difficult to achieve) with a manual system. An illustration is the monitoring of appraisal ratings discussed in Chapter 6; this could be done virtually at the touch of a button were the information recorded on a computer.

Computers in career planning

Some development work on this topic has been undertaken in educational settings, but applications in business organizations and the like are rare. In what ways can computers be used to assist in career planning and development? Answers to this question depend partly on whose perspective you take. From a personnel manager's point of view, one possible usage is to identify qualified candidates when a position needs to be filled. Searching paper records can be extremely time-consuming, but, with the appropriate data stored electronically, the search can be made very rapidly. An organization's succession planning system can readily be computerized, and there are other institutional applications of this kind. Development work undertaken by a large American corporation provides a particularly interesting illustration of what can be done.

The company was concerned to help its staff take more charge of their careers, if this was what they wanted to do. The company also wanted to improve its vacancy-filling procedures by achieving a better match between this organizational need and the needs of individuals as represented by their expressed preferences. To help people take more charge of their careers, the company devised three workbooks concerned, respectively, with self-assessment, goal-setting, and identifying career opportunities. After working through the booklets, individuals completed a form to record work preferences, either in terms of a work activity or a particular position. The information provided this way (basic biographical and career history data were included) can be entered into the company's computer. This is used to search for suitable replacements – the search being made through employees' preferences and information provided by line managers – whenever a vacancy is to be filled. The actual filling of the vacancy would be done through the company's normal staffing procedures. (A fuller account of this programme can be found in Williams, 1981).[32]

Providing career information by computer
Clearly, the potential in such a system as that just described is that it is orientated towards management's needs, and at the same time it allows individuals, if they wish to do so, to express their preferences about the next step which they see their careers taking. Potentially, therefore, it allows scope for maintaining balance between these two sets of needs, the essential feature of manpower planning. The approach also recognizes that one kind of career information is that which comes *from* the individual employee.

Another kind of information is that which the organization provides to employees; there are often inadequacies in the flow of information in this direction.

Computers offer enormous potential as a tool for providing career information. If an organization has introduced a career planning information system which includes historical data, it at least has the basis for providing information about typical career paths which employees have followed in the past. And the sort of information held in paper systems can be computerized too. But, of course, the information has to be made available to those who need it for career development purposes. Those who need direct access to career information include employees themselves and not just personnel and training staff. The use of computers to provide career information is a relatively straightforward application; more innovative still is to use the computer to support career counselling. Some development work on this has been done in the US Army, with encouraging results, as Example 8.5. shows.

Example 8.5   *Computer-aided career guidance: development work in the US army*[33]

A computer-based officer career information and planning system was developed to the stage of preliminary field testing. The US Army perceived a need for a cost-effective career counselling system to meet the two-fold aims of (a) implementing the officer career development system and (b) providing officers themselves and their career development managers with computerized information about officers' careers.

In addition, the development work can be seen as a response to complaints from officers about the existing system which failed to provide readily available, consistent, complete and current information about career progression for officers. Other evidence suggested that the interests and abilities of officers could be better used and that some inefficient career-decisions were being made.

Thus, the Army hoped to derive a number of benefits from a computer-based system:

- Greater ability of an officer to take responsibility for his or her own career decision-making.

- Greater officer satisfaction and increased knowledge of the career enhancing potentialities of various assignments.

- Better match of officer to job, based on the consideration of aptitudes, values, interests, education, training and experiences.

- More equity and efficiency in the career management system.

A number of criteria were laid down to guide the development of the system:

- It should permit the officer to explore career-related values and strategies for implementing those values.

- It should advocate flexibility in career planning.

- The dialogue between the individual and the computer should appear as natural as a conversation between an individual and a human counsellor.

- The dialogue should be designed to increase the individual's awareness of the notion of a career as a time-ordered sequence of positions, mediated partly by his or her own choices.

The design of the system provided for four 'conversational dialogue units', or modules, and there was a fifth sub-module. The first module, called 'Foresight', serves to introduce the individual to long-term career planning. 'Overview', the second module, provides information, including the Army's overall plan for officer progression, and it attempts to make the user aware of factors which can influence the development of an officer's career. These factors include:

Changes in needs, goals, and objectives of the Army
Military and technological changes
Timing of career decisions
Officer evaluation reports
Military education
Alternative specialty assignments
Civilian education and training

The third module, 'Self-assessment', aims to help users clarify what they want in terms of skills and values. Translating aspirations into long-term goals and goals into action plans for immediate objectives is the purpose of the fourth module, 'Career Strategies'. This enshrines a goal- setting philosophy, as follows:

- Goals provide the basis for long-term planning.

- Goals are arrived at by assessing the structure of Army career opportunities and by assessing one's own characteristics.

- Long-term goals can only be obtained by achieving immediate objectives.

- Concrete plans for achieving intermediate objectives provide the link between career planning and intelligent action.

The sub-module is called 'Alternative Specialty'. The officer career development system is such that officers are required to gain and maintain proficiency in two of a number of defined areas of specialization. In the eighth year of service the officer has the opportunity of choosing the second, or alternative, specialty. Subsequent career progression would normally be based on rotation of assignments between the two specialities. The sub-module therefore contains data about the various fields of specialization, how they are assigned, and how career plans can influence them.

There has been a field test of 'Foresight', 'Overview' and 'Alternative Specialty', with encouraging results. The content of the modules was considered to be interesting, accurate, useful and understandable. The use of a computer as a means of conveying career information was viewed very favourably and officers who had used the system in the pilot trial felt a decreased need for career information.

Thus it is clear that the potential applications of computers and other microchip technology to personnel and training are widespread. Not only are there direct applications to these functions, but the introduction of new technology elsewhere in the organization has implications for work and organization design, grading, training, manpower planning, and so on, all of which are legitimate concerns of personnel and training specialists.

Conclusion: managing career transition

The scenario outlined in this chapter is one that involves many changes. As much as it is true that tomorrow's employment policy issues are with us today, it remains the case that organizations generally have yet to face up to these issues: the typical PA and CD practices of the day do not reflect the social changes that have taken place in recent years. Career management can usefully be looked upon as an example of the management of change – after all, careers are very much about change. And our very conception of careers needs to undergo change. For organizations the implications may be summed up in the following paragraph.

An approach to manpower planning based on the notion of *balance* between organizational and individual needs is required. In the minds of many people career development is often looked on as being something for the primary benefit of the individual. Clearly this cannot be so, and it is as mistaken as the excessive bias towards organizational needs which dominates much of contemporary practice. Such a balanced approach will necessarily entail flexibility; one set of programmes will not meet all organizational and individual needs.

A shift towards greater *participation/involvement* of individuals in their career planning and decision-making will have to take place, and this will involve more sharing of career information by organizations. All of this will help to reflect the changed view of careers that is required – much less of a future-looking, advancement orientation, and with a greater emphasis on development within the present job and at the same level.

Such changes as these will call for changes in the individual too – a different attitude towards careers is particularly important. Many organizations provide training programmes concerned with the management of change, and they seem to deal with a wide range of organizational changes – everything but career change, however! Entry into the world of work for the first time has long been recognized as a particularly taxing change, and quite a number of organizations have well-developed induction programmes. Some other organizations provide assistance to help individuals cope with the transition to retirement or redundancy. While what is being done in these areas represents a start, there are other career transitions which remain virtually ignored. Moving to a new job within the organization, particularly if it is a promotion, is a very demanding transition which is scarcely less stressful than beginning work for the first time or being made redundant. However, a 'sink or swim' mentality seems to operate when it comes to mobility transitions. Yet failure to cope with the change is detrimental and costly to individual and organization alike. Given the need for more mobility within organizations in pursuit of career development goals, so, too, will the need for transition management programmes increase. Life skills teaching activities have particular relevance here, as do counselling and career/life planning workshops. These last mentioned activities are also of value as a means of increasing employee participation in career development, and they have many benefits for individuals; for example, clarifying career direction, realization of the utility of self-assessment, enhancement of personal adjustment and coping with career transition, and increased self-learning and development. These personal benefits are important for organizations too. Moreover, participative career development activities are a way of identifying individual needs which may be fed back into manpower plans, and they are a means of inducing realistic career expectations. But it is not sufficient for organizations simply to tack career planning workshops, for example, on to what is done already; integration is required. To encourage employee participation in career development, or management self-development for that matter, and then fail to provide the necessary support is just a kind of 'buck passing'. This points to the need to change the climate and culture of the organization as well as its policies and procedures; hence there is a need for an organization development approach to the management of career development.

Summary

Speculating about the future is a hazardous business, yet future planning is a necessary feature of organizational life. And future planning must, of course, extend to include the employment policies that an organization will adopt. The view has been put forward here that many of the employment policy issues of the future are with us already, and they stem from several sources. Career attitudes and patterns have changed, but there is, nonetheless, a need for a still greater shift away from the 'upward and onward' view of a career to a view which is more in keeping with the labour market of today and tomorrow. The labour force has changed, with a marked increase in the proportion of women. Though moderating, employees' career expectations remain too high for the prevailing low growth economy. Ways of handling redundancy and of coping with career discontent through manpower planning are examined, and the need to balance internal and external mobility and promotions is discussed. As well as social change, technological change has an impact upon employment policy. New computer-based technology also has a part to play in the operation of personnel policies, including such area as personnel information systems, career planning, and providing career information. Throughout this chapter the emphasis has been on the actions that organizations can take to match their appraisal and career development practices to the employment issues of today and tomorrow.

References

1   C. Leicester, 'Future employment issues: A survey of business opinions', *Journal of General Management*, **8** (1982) pp. 84–92.
2   Y. Guerrier and N. Philpot, *The British Manager: Career and Mobility*, Management Survey Report No. 39 (British Institute of Management 1978).
3   R. Rapoport and R.N. Rapoport, with Z. Strelitz, *Leisure and the Family Life Cycle* (Routledge and Kegan Paul 1975).
4   P. Evans and F. Bartolemé, *Must Success Cost So Much?* (Grant McIntyre 1980).
5   T. Kitwood, Disclosures *To a Stranger: Adolescent Values in an Advanced Industrial Society*, (Routledge and Kegan Paul 1980).
6   C. Hakim, *Occupational Segregation*, Research Paper No. 9 (Department of Employment 1979).
7   J. M. Adams, 'A re-entry and retainer scheme for career orientated women: National Westminster Bank Ltd', in C.L. Cooper (ed.), *Practical Approaches to Women's Career Development* (Manpower Services Commission 1982).
8   R.S. Williams, *et al.*, 'International review of staff appraisal practices: Current trends and issues', *Public Personnel Management* (January/February 1977), pp. 5–12.
9   B.M. Bass and P.C. Burger in collaboration with R. Doktor and G.V. Barrett Assessment of Managers: An International Comparison (The Free Press 1979).
10   R.L.Tung 'Selection and Training of Personnel for overseas assignments', *Columbia Journal of World Business* (Spring 1981), pp. 68–78
       R.L. Tung 'Selection and Training Procedures of US, European, and Japanese multinationals', *California Management Review*, **25** (1982), pp. 57–71.
11   Guerrier and Philpot, *The British Manager*
12   P. Warr and T.D. Wall, *Work and Well-Being* (Penguin 1975).
       T.D. Wall and C.W. Clegg, 'Who Wants Participation?', in D. Guest and K. Knight (eds), *Putting Participation Into Practice* (Gower 1979).
13   C.W. Routledge and C.K. Elliot, 'Organisational Mobility and Career Development', *Personnel Review*, **11** (1982), pp. 11–17.
14   C.B. Handy, *Understanding Organisations* 3rd edn) (Penguin 1985).
15   J. Bramham, *Human Resource Planning* (Institute of Personnel Management 1989).
16   W. Hirsh, *Succession Planning: Current Practice and Future Issues* (Institute of Manpower Studies 1990).
17   P. Swinburne, 'Unemployment in 1980', *Employee Relations*, **3** (1981).
18   J. Hayes, 'Changing the individual as a strategy for ameliorating the effects of unemployment', *Personnel Review*, **11** (1982), pp. 26–32.

19 Described in R. Hutt, *Policies for Career Change* (Institute of Manpower Studies 1981).
20 Institute of Personnel Management, *Executive Redundancy*, IPM Information Report No. 30 (Institute of Personnel Management 1980).
21 L. Clarke, *The Transition from School to Work: A Critical Review of Research in the United Kingdom* (HMSO 1980).
22 D. Parsons and R. Hutt, *The Mobility of Young Graduates* (Institute of Manpower Studies 1981).
23 K.N. Wexley and G.P. Latham, *Developing and Training Human Resources in Organizations*. Foresman Scott, Glenview, Ill. (1981).
24 J.P. Wanous, *Organizational Entry: Recruitment, Selection and Socialization of Newcomers* (Addison-Wesley 1980).
25 N. Nicholson and M. West, *Managerial Job Change: Men and Women in Transition* (Cambridge 1988).
26 M. Cross, 'Making a new career during the recession', *Employment Gazette* (June 1982), pp. 233–6.
27 Described in R. Williams, *Career Management and Career Planning* (HMSO 1981)
28 Y. Guerrier and K. MacMillan, 'Developing managers in a low-growth organization', *Personnel Management* (December, 1978), pp. 34–38.
29 J. Walker and R.S. Williams, 'Interchange scheme between the Civil Service and industry and commerce: A qualitative assessment' (Management and Personnel Office 1981).
30 J. Stinson and J. Stokes, 'How to multi-appraise', *Management Today* (June 1980), pp. 43, 45, 46, 48, 53.
31 A. Evans, *Computerizing Personnel Systems* (Institute of Personnel Management 1986).
   M.L. Gallagher, *Computers and Personnel Management* (Heinemann 1986).
32 Williams, *Career Management and Career Planning*.
33 Described in Williams, *Career Management and Career Planning*.

9
Some final thoughts

During the 1960s, performance appraisal practices developed and broadened very much in tune with society's development generally. That development continued into the 1970s but by the end of the decade things were becoming rather more static. With society's problems in the early 1980s, the danger is that we may start slipping into reverse. Just as when individuals encounter complicated and stressful circumstances, which are difficult to cope with, they often regress to less mature, simpler and more dependent ways of behaving, so organizations and even society as a whole may reflect the same tendency in the face of world recession. Sometimes this surfaces in the form of statements about 'needing to re-establish basic values', but it generally comes down to the same thing – trying to put the clock back. It can constantly be seen in organizational appraisal schemes. For example, the suggestion by at least one major employer that it will use appraisal data in helping decide whom to make redundant is a reversion to the carrot and stick (minus the carrot) approach which characterized appraisals several years ago. It would probably have much the same effect – that is, a bad effect – as has repeatedly been found when linking pay to performance appraisal.

Economically, the clock has of course been put back a fair amount. The fallacy is to think that everything else has moved in the same direction. Social attitudes and expectations may re-adjust to some extent, but it seems very unlikely that they will go back to something akin to what one would have found in the 1930s, or even the 1950s. There is going to be a continuing, maybe even increasing, demand for participation; women are not going to be content to stay at home; educational levels will remain high; and so on. Organizations seeking to adapt to difficult economic circumstances by, amongst other things, opting for more primitive appraisal schemes are simply storing up trouble for themselves. It is as important for appraisal and career development practices to be socially attuned and relevant as for them to be economically relevant.

Some adaptation of existing practices will surely be necessary. It is not just a question of responding to a changed environment, but there is also a need to improve on present approaches. During the course of this book, we have described or reviewed numerous techniques used in the field; all have their imperfections. The difficulty is in deciding which general approach seems the most sensible in the circumstances. Some help in resolving this may be derived from the increasing understanding of human judgemental processes provided by research. Whereas much of the earlier investigation of the problems of appraisal centred on the types of rating scale available and how they were used, more recent work has focused on the appraiser's causal attributions – the way in which he or she tends to explain the cause of good or bad performance. Before we take a look at this, you might like to think back to one or two instances when you did something rather badly at work. Why did it happen? When you have thought abut this, recall some instance of poor performance on the part of a subordinate (or, indeed, almost anyone else) and now say why that happened. The chances are that, when you explained your own poor performance you made reference to situational and circumstantial factors as being the main cause. This is what would be called an *external* attribution. When explaining other people's behaviour, as in the case of your subordinate, we have a more marked tendency to see it as being brought about by characteristics of the person rather than of the situation. In other words we make an *internal* attribution. This tendency to take more account of the situation in explaining our own behaviour and less account of it in explaining other people's is sometimes called the 'fundamental attributional error'.[1]

Now, while all that has been said so far about our attributions is generally true, things are of course a bit more complicated than this. When we explain performance in terms of internal factors, it is most often by reference to either effort or ability. When we explain it by external factors most often we refer to either luck or the difficulty of the task. How we apply these explanations to people and events is partly determined by our attitudes and feelings towards the individuals or groups concerned. This is illustrated in a study by Garland and Price[2] which found that successful performance of female managers was attributed by prejudiced male managers to luck and an easy task, but by unprejudiced male managers to skill and hard work. The consequences of the person's behaviour affects our attributions too; one study[3] showed that when the consequences of poor performance were major, supervisors made more internal causal attributions for that performance. Other work in this field has demonstrated that if supervisors attribute subordinates' performance (be it good or bad) to the *effort* displayed by the subordinates, they make more extreme evaluations of that performance than if they attribute it to subordinates' ability.[4]

So, while we have a tendency to make more external attributions for our own behaviour and more internal attributions for other people's, this is much modified according to whether we are talking about good or bad performance, whether we are assessing people we have a positive attitude towards, the consequences of the performance, and numerous other factors. What does all this mean in terms of performance appraisal? It is hard to disagree with Knowlton and Mitchell[5] when they conclude:

> 'If leaders or supervisors make attributions for subordinate behaviour that are subject to motivational or informational biases, and these attributions affect performance evaluations, then their behaviour may be inappropriate and may have a substantial influence on the satisfaction and motivation of subordinates and the effectiveness of the organization.'

More research is needed on these biases and their nature, but what is clear is that they exist and that they are substantial and pervasive. Something can be done in training appraisers to increase their awareness of these distortions – exercises for doing this are easily devised – but it is questionable whether this would ever suffice to eradicate them.

If it is accepted that we are unlikely to overcome all the problems of the subjectivity of an appraiser's judgement, the question arises as to where we go from here and what the alternatives are. One answer is to just soldier on; there is, after all, some evidence that performance feedback can have beneficial effects when handled properly, despite the questionable nature of the underlying assessment. However, the fact that it is possible for some appraisers to manage this does not mean that they all will, even given ideal circumstances – and ideal circumstances are hardly the norm. Alternatively, one can opt for a results-orientated approach, which (if used by itself) means putting aside the administrative functions of appraisal, that is, using it as a mechanism for making comparisons and for the fair allocation of rewards, etc. There is a great deal to be said for paying less attention to the administrative purposes and concentrating on making appraisal useful for the parties most directly involved, though some doubt does remain as to whether the goal-setting approach adequately meets the appraisee's need for feedback. If the assessment and feedback functions of appraisal – and their implied value for administrative decision-making – are deemed to be indispensable, the conclusion drawn earlier about the fallibilities of human judgement strongly implies that the traditional 'father'-based assessment is too often inaccurate and unfair. There would seem to be an increasingly strong case for the use of multiple appraisal, or at least dual assessment involving both the appraiser's ratings and the appraisee's self-ratings. As Brinkerhoff and Kanter say:[6]

> '. . . single measurement systems based on formal checklists and ratings by the supervisor should be confined only to those more routinized tasks

in organizations . . . As uncertainty grows – or complexity, interdependence, power concerns and/or multiple appraisal concerns grow – then so should the number of additional features and sources of data added to appraisal systems.'

There is good evidence[7] for thinking that the multiple-rater approach has considerable advantages, but it may prove too complex or time-consuming for many organizations. The incorporation of more self-assessment in the appraisal process is not, however, over-difficult to achieve. It is not the intention to review this topic all over again, as it has already been covered. But, as was said then, it is *also* worth considering an approach based heavily on self-appraisal as an alternative to goal-setting, where the comparability function of appraisal is dispensed with.

Some of the difficulties inherent in the common approaches to appraisal stem from the practice of linking appraisal of performance with appraisal of potential, both in terms of time and documentation. As was indicated in the last chapter, the present economic circumstances have forced many organizations into a process of contraction, thus reducing career prospects; even some degree of recovery and growth in industry is unlikely to return us to our original position in the foreseeable future. But one small benefit that arises from this is that it allows us, potentially, to eliminate some of the problems encountered in appraising potential. With fewer promotions on offer, it is less worthwhile incorporating this element into the annual appraisal. Moreover, while appraisers might be even more inclined to give over-optimistic potential ratings to their more promising subordinates to give them a chance in the face of limited opportunities, the fact that they are so limited makes it even more important for the organization not only to get their promotions right but *to be seen* to be getting them right. It was argued earlier that this might lead to an increased use of assessment centre methods – they certainly have high 'face validity'. Given the combination of circumstances, it is difficult to believe that ACs will not increasingly be deployed. One further point is worth remembering here; taking assessments of potential out of the context of annual performance appraisal should make it easier to introduce self-appraisal and other more participative approaches.

Restricted career prospects have an impact on career development activities and policies, quite apart from the methods used for assessing potential. Some of the more likely effects were reviewed in the course of Chapter 8. The need to respond to the changed circumstances by providing more forms of development other than just vertical progress should not be underestimated. The initial psychological approach to a thwarted need, to frustration, is very often a constructive and adaptive one; the individual frequently continues to seek the goal being sought but with intensified effort. However, the next stage beyond this is anything but useful in organizational terms. If the individual experiences prolonged frustration – if, despite his efforts, no reward is forthcoming – he may conclude that he has little or no control over important aspects of his working life, and the psychological consequence of this is generally apathy, withdrawal and loss of self-esteem. Such people learn to become helpless – they give up making any effort even when there is a change in circumstances and their efforts might now be rewarded.

The more immediate consequences of not providing sufficient outlets for career development needs, then, may not be too detrimental to the effectiveness of the organization – but the longer-term response may be very damaging indeed. Having dissatisfied managers is undesirable, but having apathetic and unresponsive ones is a great deal worse. Lowered self-esteem is not something to be taken lightly, because, over and over again, self-esteem is found to correlate with performance.[8] There is evidence for believing that these negative effects of failing to provide career development opportunities are going to get worse, not just because of diminished prospects, but because of the improved educational level of much of the white-collar workforce. Klein and Maher[9] found that, within each job level, the greater the educational qualifications an individual had, the more likely he was to have low job satisfaction. It seems that the general increase in the amount of education people have – quite apart from the propensity to recruit over-qualified staff in times of recession (when they cannot find appropriate jobs to go for) – will tend to increase expectations that are hard to meet, at least in any one job over a long period.

Looking at this picture overall, it would seem that the need to employ the kinds of self-development techniques outlined in Chapter 4 is considerable. What was said about the role of the line manager and about counselling and mobility policies is very relevant here too. The aim should perhaps be not just to provide career development outlets of various kinds, but to provide them in such a way as to maximize the individual manager's sense of personal control over his or her working life.[10] Doing so will benefit both him or her and the organization.

Finally, whatever policies or methods are implemented in the area of appraisal and development, it should be emphasized again that consultation and evaluation are needed all the way down the line in the process, otherwise what emerges may be very different from what was intended. Simply formulating a sound proposal for an appraisal system is not enough; nor is it a guarantee of things working well if you involve the appraising managers in the planning (though it may well guarantee the collapse of the whole thing if you do not). The monitoring and evaluation process has to be designed to bring home to those involved that appraisal is important and will be taken seriously. As Brewster and Richbell[11] say: 'managers are only likely to adjust their priorities if there is some indicator of a change in the importance their superiors have given existing policies or some sign that a new policy is highly regarded.' In practice, this means proper training and resourcing, inclusion of appraisal and development of subordinates as a feature of the manager's own appraisal, central monitoring of appraisal with some come-back on managers who fall short on their responsibilities in this area, and so forth.

But this brings us back to the very basic question of whether top management see appraisal as being worthwhile anyway. If they do not see it to devote time and resources to appraising and developing employee performance, they will pay a high price when the employees draw the obvious conclusion.

References

1 L. Ross, 'The intuitive psychologist and his shortcomings: distortions in the attribution process', *Advances in Experimental Social Psychology*, Vol. 10 (1977).
2 H. Garland and K.H. Price, 'Attitudes toward women in management and attributions of their success and failure in managerial positions', *Journal of Applied Psychology*, **62**, (1977), pp. 29–33.
3 T.R. Mitchell and R.E. Wood, 'Supervisors responses to subordinate poor performance: a test of an attribution model' *Organizational Behaviour and Human Performance*, **25** (1980), pp. 123–38.
4 W.A. Knowlton and T.R. Mitchell, 'Effects of causal attributions on a supervisor's evaluation of subordinate performance', *Journal of Applied Psychology*, **65** (1980), pp. 459–66.
5 ibid.
6 D.W. Brinkerhoff and R.M. Kanter, 'Appraising the performance of performance appraisal', *Sloan Management Review*, **21** (1980), pp. 3–16.
7 E.E. Lawler, 'The multitrait-multirater approach to measuring managerial job performance', *Journal of Applied Psychology*, **57** (1967) pp. 369–81.
8 A.K. Korman, 'Toward a hypothesis of work behavior', *Journal of Applied Psychology*, **54** (1970), pp. 31–41
A.K. Korman, 'Hypotheses of work behavior revisited, and an extension', *Academy of Management Review* **1** (1976), pp. 50–63.
9 S.M. Klein and J.R. Maher, 'Educational level and satisfaction with pay', *Personnel Psychology*, **19** (1966), pp. 195–208.
10 G.C. Thornton, 'Differential effects of career planning on internals and externals', *Personnel Psychology*, **31** (1978), pp. 471–76.
11 C.J. Brewster and S. Richbell, 'Getting managers to implement personnel policies', *Personnel Management* (December 1982), pp. 34–37.

Appendix A

An example of an evaluation questionnaire sent to appraisers (the questionnaire is pre-coded for computer analysis)

			1–3

Questionnaire to appraisers

Please record your answers to the questions on this page by putting a tick in the appropriate box on the right.

1 How many staff have you given an appraisal interview to:

		4/5

2 Have you yourself ever been given an appraisal interview?

Yes		1	6
No		2	

3 How much time (on average) did you spend in preparing for each of the interviews?

Less than $\frac{1}{2}$ hour		1
$\frac{1}{2}$ hour but less than 1 hour		2	7
1 hour but less than 2 hours		3
2 hours or more		4

4 When giving the interviews, did you generally find any difficulty in getting the interviewees to:

	Yes	No	Did not try to get them to	
Talk freely				8
Comment on their own performance weaknesses				9
Put forward their own solutions to problems				10
Discuss their working relationship with colleagues				11
	1	2	3	

152

5 Did you usually find that the interviewee did most
of the talking in the interview?

Yes		1
No		2

12

6 Do you feel that the appraisees were being frank with you in the interview?

Yes, all of them		1
Yes, most of them		2
Yes, some of them		3
None of them		4

13

7 Did any of the appraisals you conducted make you aware of any staff problems or job problems (e.g. lack of clear job definition, too heavy or too light workload) that you had not previously known about?

	Yes	No	
Made me aware of staff problems			14
Made me aware of job problems			15
	1	2	

8 Did anything you learned in the appraisal cause you to modify your assessment of the interviewee?

Yes, in one or more cases		1
Never		2

16

9 Do you think that the appraisals have, either directly or indirectly, led to an improvement in the job performance of the interviewees?

Yes, in every case		1
Yes, in some cases		2
No		3
Too soon to tell		4

17

10 Generally speaking, do you think you got anything useful out of the appraisals you gave?

Yes		1
No		2

18

11 Do you feel that the appraisal interview fits in with your normal style of management?

Yes		1
No		2

19

12 How do you, as a manager, feel about performance appraisal interviews?

I am greatly in favour of them	☐	1
I am in favour of them	☐	2
I am indifferent to them	☐	3 20
I am against them	☐	4
I am strongly against them	☐	5

13 Who do you think benefits most from the appraisal, the interviewer or the interviewee?

The interviewer, usually	☐	1
The interviewee, usually	☐	2
Both benefit to some extent	☐	3 21
Neither benefits	☐	4

14 Are you satisfied that the appraisal action sheet is adequate for conveying the action recommendations that come out of the interviews?

Yes	☐	1
No	☐	2 22

Thank you for your co-operation

Appendix B

An example of an evaluation questionnaire sent to appraisees (the questionnaire is pre-coded for computer analysis)

CONFIDENTIAL

| | | | | 1–4

1 What was the grade of your appraisal interviewer?

If he is a member of a specialist or professional group (e.g. an engineer) please state what discipline he belongs to here:	For Office Use Only
	☐ 5
Where boxes are placed for your use, please put a tick (✓) in the one which is appropriate for you.	☐ 6

2 How many times have you been given an appraisal interview?

Once	☐ 1	
Twice	☐ 2	7
Three or more times	☐ 3	

(If you have been given more than one, please relate your answers to the most recent one.)

3 How long is it since you last had an appraisal?

Less than 1 month	☐ 1	
1 month but less than 3 months	☐ 2	
3 months but less than 6 months	☐ 3	8
6 months or more	☐ 4	

4 How much advance warning were you given that you were going to be interviewed?

No advance warning	☐ 1	
Less than 1 day	☐ 2	
1 day but less than 3 days	☐ 3	9
3 days or more	☐ 4	

155

5 Did you make use of the interview preparation form?

Yes ☐ 1

No ☐ 2

10

6 How long did the interview last?

Less than $\frac{1}{2}$ hour ☐ 1

$\frac{1}{2}$–1 hour ☐ 2

Over 1 hour ☐ 3

11

7 Did the interviewer mention any parts of the job you had done particularly well?

Yes ☐ 1

No ☐ 2

12

8 Was there any mention or discussion of the weaker aspects of your performance in the job during the interview?

Yes ☐ 1

No ☐ 2

13

9 Do you feel that the interviewer had made a reasonably fair assessment of your performance in the job?

Yes ☐ 1

No ☐ 2

14

10 What impression did you get of how the interviewer considered your performance in the job? That he thought it was:

Outstanding ☐ 1

Very good ☐ 2

Good ☐ 3

Fair ☐ 4

Not quite adequate ☐ 5

Unsatisfactory ☐ 6

(Got no impression at all) ☐ 7

15

11 In some appraisal interviews the person being interviewed or the interviewer, may raise the topic of promotion. Were your promotion prospects discussed in the interview?

Yes ☐ 1

No ☐ 2

16

If 'YES', what impression did you get of your promotion prospects in the very near future? That they were:

Very good	☐	1
Good	☐	2 17
Not good	☐	3

12 Were your training needs mentioned or discussed in the interview?

Yes	☐	1
No	☐	2 18

13 Did you get the impression that the interviewer was being completely frank with you in the interview?

Yes	☐	1
No	☐	2 19

14 Two kinds of appraisal interview are described below. Different people find different sorts of interview most useful to them personally. Which one of these would *you* find preferable?

Interview *A*   The interviewer tells you what he feels your strengths and weaknesses are and what you can do to improve your performance. He explains the basis for this assessment and encourages you to accept the line of action proposed.

☐   20

Interview *B*   You are asked by the interviewer to review your own performance in the past year and to suggest ways in which it can be improved. The interviewer presses you for ideas on how to solve any difficulties you have encountered in the job.

☐   21

Thinking back to the last interview you were given, which of these two types of interview did it most resemble?

Very similar to Interview *A*	☐	1
Slightly similar to Interview *A*	☐	2
Not like either of them	☐	3 22
Slightly similar to Interview *B*	☐	4
Very similar to Interview *B*	☐	5

15 Did any firm proposals for action (e.g. changing your work methods, giving you more responsibility or guidance, recommending a transfer, etc.) come out of the appraisal?

Yes   ☐ 1
No   ☐ 2   23

16 Did the interview make you feel that you *wanted* to improve your performance in the job?

Yes   ☐ 1
No   ☐ 2   24
I did not get the impression that there was any real need to   ☐ 3

17 After the appraisal, were you any clearer in your own mind about what you could do to improve your work?

Yes   ☐ 1
No   ☐ 2   25

18 Do you think the appraisal interview has led to, or is likely to lead to, any improvement in your job performance?

Yes, a considerable improvement   ☐ 1
Yes, a slight improvement   ☐ 2
Neither improvement nor deterioration   ☐ 3   26
No, a slight deterioration   ☐ 4
No, a considerable deterioration   ☐ 5

19 Has the fact that you have had an appraisal interview affected your general satisfaction with the job?

It has greatly increased my satisfaction   ☐ 1
It has slightly increased my satisfaction   ☐ 2
It has not affected my satisfaction   ☐ 3   27
It has slightly decreased my satisfaction   ☐ 4
It has greatly decreased my satisfaction   ☐ 5

20 How do you feel about performance appraisals?

I am strongly in favour of them   ☐ 1
I am slightly in favour of them   ☐ 2
I am neither for nor against them   ☐ 3   28
I am slightly against them   ☐ 4
I am strongly against them   ☐ 5

21 Below are a number of statements describing various features of appraisal interviews. They are arranged in pairs, the two statements in each pair being in contrast to one another. The line which joins the two statements in each pair is divided into six sections. Please examine each statement in a pair and then decide which comes closest to describing the interview which *you* had; the better it describes your interview, the nearer that end of the line you should put your tick. (Ignore the boxes at the side of these statements.)

EXAMPLE: Please put your tick through the line like this

The interviewer was friendly ⌊__⌊__⌊ ✓ ⌊__⌊__⌋ The interviewer was hostile

The interviewer did nearly all the talking in the interview	⌊__⌊__⌊__⌊__⌊__⌋	I did most of the talking in the interview 29
The interviewer seemed wholly concerned with *assessing* my work performance over the last year	⌊__⌊__⌊__⌊__⌊__⌋	The interviewer seemed chiefly interested in *improving* my work performance in the year ahead 30
I felt it would have been best not to pursue the matter where points of disagreement arose	⌊__⌊__⌊__⌊__⌊__⌋	The interviewer made me feel that I was free to discuss points of disagreement with him 31
The interviewer did not allow me to offer my viewpoint on the way I coped with the job	⌊__⌊__⌊__⌊__⌊__⌋	The interviewer allowed me to put forward my own views on how I had coped with the job 32
The interviewer seemed to have made up his mind about things before the interview started	⌊__⌊__⌊__⌊__⌊__⌋	I got the impression that the interviewer was willing to change his views on things in the light of what I said 33

Almost all the ideas for getting round job difficulties came from the interviewer	└─┴─┴─┴─┴─┘	I provided most of the solutions to the problems we discussed

34

The interviewer made no attempt to understand my feelings about the job	└─┴─┴─┴─┴─┘	The interviewer made every attempt to understand the way I felt about the job

35

The interviewer did not appear to be paying attention when I was speaking	└─┴─┴─┴─┴─┘	The interviewer listened most attentively whenever I spoke

36

The interviewer did not invite me to put forward any ideas or suggestions about the job	└─┴─┴─┴─┴─┘	The interviewer continually pressed me for *my* ideas and suggestions about the job

37

The interviewer did not try to help me clarify my own thoughts about the job	└─┴─┴─┴─┴─┘	The interviewer tried to help me clarify my own thoughts about the job

38

Please use this space if you have any comments on, or suggestions for changes in, the appraisal scheme, or if there are any points arising out of this questionnaire which you wish to say more about.

Please check through to see that nothing has been left out. Many thanks for your help and co-operation.

If you have NOT *had an appraisal interview, please answer these few questions*

1 Do you know why you have not been given an appraisal

Yes	□	1	39
No	□	2	

2 Would you have liked to have had one?

Yes	□	1	40
No	□	2	

3 What impression have you got of how the department rates your performance in the job? That it is considered to be:

Outstanding	□	1	
Very good	□	2	
Good	□	3	
Fair	□	4	15
Not quite adequate	□	5	
Unsatisfactory	□	6	
(Got no impression at all)	□	7	

4 Have you been in your present post for less than one year?

Yes	□	1	42
No	□	2	

Appendix C

Example of a covering note sent out with the appraisees' evaluation questionnaire.

Dear Colleague,

Will you help, please?

This questionnaire is part of a study of appraisal interviews being carried out in a number of departments in (name of organization). The aims of the study are to assess how well the scheme is working, to find out what people who have themselves been interviewed think of it, and finally to consider what improvements might be made. To help us obtain the information we need, we would be grateful if you would answer this questionnaire, a copy of which is being sent to staff who may receive interviews. (If you have *not* been given one yet, please just answer the questions on the back of the questionnaire.) The trade union representatives concerned have seen the questionnaire and have agreed to co-operate in this study. Given your help, the results of the survey should be of benefit to all concerned. The report of the study will be made available to both management and unions.

Please be completely frank in answering this questionnaire. The procedure for distributing it has been so designed as to ensure the anonymity of the replies. It is easy to complete and should not take long to do. When you have finished, return it in the envelope provided.

Finally, please do not consult anyone else when answering these questions; it is *your* personal opinions we are interested in.

Thank you for your co-operation.

Index